Effective Work Management

MILON BROWN

THE MACMILLAN COMPANY   *New York*

First printing

Library of Congress Catalog Card Number: 60–13223

The Macmillan Company, New York
Brett-Macmillan Ltd., Galt, Ontario

Printed in the United States of America

Preface

The management of any enterprise is a complex undertaking because it deals with many different factors of group activity. Management must consider *people* who are often careless and unpredictable; *machines* of great value and intricacy; *materials* that are constantly changing as new discoveries are made; *money*, often in frightening quantities; and *production methods* that must be kept at high efficiency.

The possible relationships between these factors are infinite, and no one book could cover the subject adequately. Still, many persons want, and are entitled to, a brief explanation of the principles that are used as guides to the efficient handling of these elements in business and other institutions.

I have tried to present these principles while avoiding detailed discussion of the most complex element of all, the human one; and by limiting coverage of financial management to the aspects that directly affect work. A far less involved treatment was made possible by eliminating these two factors and concentrating on work management. My primary goal was to present a nontechnical view of the basic management processes as they operate in the job situation, a primer of management, so to speak.

In keeping with this goal, I have tried to use everyday language instead of technical terms. Where it has been necessary to introduce expressions with special meanings, they have been defined. To further facilitate understanding, I used the principle of repetition extensively. Many of the ideas I con-

v

sider essential have been introduced in several different parts of the text to emphasize their importance and reinforce their grasp by the reader.

I believe a clear understanding of the total management concept will be particularly helpful to young men and women who hope to become executives. Some may still be in school, others employed. For the latter, this understanding will probably be most valuable to those in middle or lower management positions. Executives at higher levels may find the discussion interesting and helpful as a summary of modern management philosophy. Some may want to use it to develop the managerial competence of promising subordinates. A major responsibility of executives today is to encourage and promote the growth of their employees in the knowledge and skill needed in the organization.

In planning the contents, certain assumptions had to be made. For instance, I feel that persons who want to become skillful managers will make better progress if they comprehend the managerial processes *before* they assume responsibilities at a higher level. In other words, the skills needed by a manager are developed faster if the person understands his relationships to the basic processes. Even more basic assumptions are that effective management can be learned and that normal adults can learn it. Finally it was concluded that the processes were not so complex that verbal description would be impracticable.

The real purpose of the book is to help the reader understand what is meant by "management" in connection with work. Because the management processes are dynamic and much remains to be discovered about them, they can only be described here as they are generally understood and accepted today with the hope that the reader will keep abreast of future progress.

DATE DUE

MAR 26 1987		BIRD	
DEC 09 1987		NOV 23 1987 RET	
MAY 3 1988		BIRD	
		APR 20 '88 RET	
NOV 02 1989			
NOV 30 1989		NOV 02 1989 RET	
		DEC 11 1989 RET	
		APR 30 1990 RET	
MAY 01 1990			
		MAR 24 1987	

Effective Work Management

THE MACMILLAN COMPANY
NEW YORK · CHICAGO
DALLAS · ATLANTA · SAN FRANCISCO
LONDON · MANILA

IN CANADA
BRETT-MACMILLAN LTD.
GALT, ONTARIO

The book is written to provide information rather than to increase managerial skills: No book can develop skills because "we learn to *do* by *doing*" and not by reading. This does not mean, however, that the text is not practical or useful. Careful study of the contents should make the acquisition of skills and competence much easier. In addition it should lay the groundwork for superior performance in the management of tomorrow, where sound leadership will be all-important. Current trends indicate that in the future the use of authority will be replaced by ethical methods of persuasion, and many difficult problems will be solved by the integration of conflicting goals.

Some management skill may be developed, but any increase in ability is incidental to the primary purpose which is understanding the implications of the management cycle as it operates in business situations. The goal, then, is to provide a sound basis upon which either an individual or a company can build an effective program of executive development to secure sound management practices within the enterprise.

MILON BROWN

Contents

Contents

PART ONE

The Meaning
of Management

To secure a clear understanding of a new subject, it is necessary to create a sound frame of reference by putting the important background facts in their proper perspective. Part One presents the foundation of ideas upon which the rest of the book is based; it sets the limits of the discussion and introduces the student to the concept of work management.

1

What a Manager Does

ORIGIN OF MANAGEMENT

Although the practice of management, like the art of organization, has ancient roots, management did not become a scientific concept until the beginning of the twentieth century. During the first 150 years after the industrial revolution, the emphasis was still on how to make the products. Supervisors gained their knowledge of managing capital, plants, equipment, materials, and people by experience. Management was primarily based on common sense and experience, and knowledge of a particular branch of business was, and sometimes still is, the sole criterion of competence.

Most business managers gained their experience from long and unorganized apprenticeships. They concentrated on things and processes rather than on the ways people work together. To them, the machines were "tools," and the new and larger business enterprises, brought about by the machines, were organized as enlarged forms of master craftsmanship.

At the turn of the century, Frederick W. Taylor, an industrial engineer, introduced scientific management as a branch of knowledge. Although successful management was already

3

a familiar phenomenon and there had been some attempts to apply scientific concepts to management, it was Taylor who established definitely that management is an art, with its own principles and methods and separate from the technology of manufacturing.

He first conceived the idea of scientific management while solving the day-to-day problems in his work at Midvale Steel Co., Bethlehem Steel Co., and other firms between 1880 and 1900. His papers and book on the subject are now classics.[1]

Taylor saw the need for a systematic and scientific approach to industrial management. The prevailing methods of leadership and work performance were haphazard and inefficient. At that time, managers used personal leadership and special inducements such as piece work, premium pay, or bonus plans to secure production results.

Taylor's revolutionary proposals for bringing system and order to the work with scientific management are commonplace today. He advocated that managers "take over all work for which they are better fitted than the workmen," and that the "new types of work done by management" would make "scientific management so much more efficient than the old plan."[2]

[1] "A Piece Rate System," Paper No. 647, Transactions of ASME, XVI, 1895, p. 856.

"Shop Management" (1903); Paper No. 1003, Transactions of ASME, XXII, Harper and Brothers, New York, 1911, p. 1337.

"On the Art of Cutting Metals" (Presidential Address, 1906); Paper No. 1119, Transactions of ASME, XXVIII, p. 31.

The Principles of Scientific Management, privately printed and distributed to members of ASME, Harper and Brothers, New York, 1911, 1942, 1947.

Testimony at Hearings before Special Committee of the House of Representatives to Investigate the Taylor and Other Systems of Shop Management under authority of H. Res. 90. Government Printing Office, Washington, 1912.

[2] Frederick Winslow Taylor, *The Principles of Scientific Management,* Harper and Brothers, New York, 1911, 1942, 1947, p. 36.

Instead of letting workers learn their skills by watching others and developing their abilities in any fashion they wanted, Taylor suggested that managers condense the great mass of traditional knowledge to a science by "classifying, tabulating, and reducing this knowledge to rules, laws and formulae." [3] Managers could then train workmen to use these standardized methods instead of permitting each to choose his own way.

He also recommended that managers plan the work of the people reporting to them and devise means to coordinate and control. As he put it, "The work of every workman is fully planned out by the management at least one day in advance, and each man receives in most cases complete written instructions, describing in detail the task which he is to accomplish, as well as the means to be used in doing the work. . . . This task specifies not only what is to be done, but how it is to be done and the exact time allowed for doing it." [4]

Under Taylor's plan, managers would motivate their people not by standing to one side and giving orders but by selecting, teaching, and developing the workmen and cooperating with them.

Much of the current thinking on management is firmly established on Taylor's ideas: the need to systematize management, to analyze the work, to measure it, and to assign portions to the people in the organization best suited to perform it.

Taylor recognized that the person who planned the work was often ill-equipped to carry it out. His initial assumption was that a pig-iron handler lacked the requisite education and would be underpaid if he had to plan his own work, and the supervisor who did the planning would be belittling his own

[3] *Ibid.*, p. 36.
[4] *Ibid.*, p. 39.

abilities and would be overpaid if he were put to pig-iron handling.

Managers, according to Taylor, should set and enforce standards and try to improve methods and cooperation, because this could not be entrusted to the people being managed. The manager should also be responsible for developing his people and rewarding them for outstanding work. Although he did not provide the whole answer to what a manager is, Taylor did help management take a long stride forward.

Since that time, a discipline of management has been developing. Although long neglected in favor of research into the technical and functional aspects of management, a basic knowledge and understanding of the business enterprise, necessary for the full development of this discipline of management, is emerging. Significant contributions have been made by business managers, public administrators, management consultants, and social scientists.

THE MEANING OF THE WORD "MANAGEMENT"

At this point it would be wise to clarify what is meant by "management." Sometimes it is used to designate the *people* who manage, such as "middle management," "top management," or simply "management," although more correctly, these people are called "managers," as done in this book. Another meaning of "management" refers to the way things are accomplished in an enterprise. More specifically, in this sense it means the effective use of people, money, equipment, materials, and methods to accomplish a specified objective. This is the generally accepted meaning and one used throughout the book.

Even though acceptance of these definitions will prevent confusion, a further analysis is worth-while at this time. As in any new field, there are many theories about the management concept. One school of thought proposes that management is the art of getting things done through people. It emphasizes the human element by stressing human relations, group dynamics, and personnel management. Another theory is that management is primarily setting objectives and making decisions to attain the objectives and that all other managerial activities are subordinated to decision-making. As mentioned above, a third group believes management concerns itself with the most efficient use of men, money, materials, machines, and methods to accomplish a specified purpose. Each of these theories has merit because each emphasizes an important component of managerial success. Here, an analysis of what goes on in the operation of an entire enterprise will be presented instead of any single aspect or process.

APPLICATION OF MANAGEMENT PRINCIPLES

Another widely discussed theory is that the same principles are applicable to any situation that requires management. Generally, this is true. The processes described in this book are basic and can be applied widely. On the other hand, there are many different ways in which these processes or principles can be used.

Today, reference is frequently made to sales management, warehouse management, inventory management, or such special applications as hotel or hospital management. Each of these areas can be studied separately. The way the management processes are applied varies somewhat according to particular needs of each. Although the fundamentals of good management are equally applicable to both private enterprise and government, business must devote attention to manufacturing, marketing, and similar activities that are seldom required in a governmental operation.

Another application should be noted. It was stated above that men, money, materials, and methods are all included in the scope of management. Employee (men) problems are in the area of personnel management; the fiscal (money) aspects of an operation concentrate on financial management. The use of materials and methods involve industrial management. This book describes the application of management principles to the work itself and, therefore, devotes more attention to the physical situations than to either people or funds.

Even though work management is emphasized, it must be recognized that all jobs, all work, and all accomplishments are done by people and it is impossible to make a sharp distinction between the personal and the impersonal elements in supervision or work management. There is no good reason to erect artificial and arbitrary barriers between these two aspects, but work-management factors rather than the human element will be emphasized.

RELATION OF MANAGEMENT TO SUPERVISION

Another word that is used loosely is "supervision." It is frequently used to indicate the job relationships that exist between a person and those who report directly to him. Thus, the president of a corporation exercises supervision over a few executives and staff officials who are immediately below him in the organization. These people, in turn, supervise their respective subordinates and so on, down to the first-level foreman or supervisor who directs the work of a small group of employees with little or no supervisory responsibility. Naturally, far less supervision is necessary at the top of an organization than at the bottom. More experienced employees usually need, and receive, less supervision. The first-level supervisor spends practically all of his time directing the work assignments of subordinates. In many companies, supervisor-development programs are planned for employees on this first level because they need more guidance and at the same time they can establish good supervisory practices early in their careers.

Every person who directs the work activities of subordinates has definite supervisory responsibilities, but ordinarily he is called a supervisor only at the lower levels. An analysis of duties and responsibilities shows that at higher levels more time is spent on planning, making decisions, getting plans implemented, and checking on the results. These are the management processes and phases and are of a somewhat different nature than directing the work of subordinates on a person-to-person basis.

RELATION OF MANAGEMENT TO ADMINISTRATION

The word "administration" is often used synonymously with "management." In recent years, however, "administration" has come to mean functions performed at the top of an organization where the primary objectives or purposes of the whole enterprise are formulated, broad policies established, and decisions made about financing, basic organizational structure, and similar central problems. The persons who make such decisions are often called "administrators." In his book, *The Art of Administration,* Ordway Tead stresses the general nature of these activities in the following words, ". . . administration is conceived as the necessary activities of those individuals (executives) in an organization who are charged with ordering, forwarding, and facilitating the associated efforts of a group of individuals brought together to realize certain defined purposes." [5]

[5] Ordway Tead, *The Art of Administration,* McGraw-Hill Book Co., Inc., New York, 1951, p. 3.

After these basic decisions have been made, they have to be carried out by executives or operating officials at the lower levels. These persons are the real managers. Their major responsibility is to get effective action that results in economical accomplishment of the objectives within the limitations of the established policies. This intermediate group has heavy responsibility for planning how to get the work done, determining who will do each part, issuing clear directions, setting quality and quantity standards, and checking on accomplishment. These are all parts of the management cycle that will be described in this chapter.

THE FIVE PRIMARY PROCESSES

From the experiences of people working to accomplish common purposes, some aspects of management have become well established. There are a number of ways in which these actions may be grouped or identified for study. For instance, in the management philosophy of the General Electric Co., the basic processes are called:

1. Planning or "management by objective"
2. Organizing (with as few layers as possible)
3. Integrating (as defined by Mary Parker Follett)
4. Measuring (including what is called the control process)

The grouping presented in the following pages is equally simple and more commonly accepted in practice today. Many students of management refer to these areas as processes of management. The word "process" is used in the same general sense as "activity." The activities engaged in by executives to manage their work assignments may be categorized as follows:

1. The planning process—thinking about the job to be done, what equipment, supplies, and space are needed to do it,

what the future may hold, formulating clear objectives, orderly plans, and decisions about how the job will be accomplished best

2. The organizing process—putting the thinking and planning into an organized structure so there is a more or less stable grouping of activities and equipment and plans can be executed effectively

3. The directing process—furnishing directions, giving instructions, and related activities to set the organization in motion and keep it moving toward achieving the goal

4. The coordinating process—timing and scheduling the work of the entire organization and gearing it into the efforts and programs of the organizational segments (and individuals) to ensure proper work flow, synchronizing activities in all units, making the best use of all efforts to achieve the purpose

5. The control process—reviewing progress in relation to goals, setting standards and checking against these standards and by other means making certain that the purposes are being attained as planned.

These five categories cover fairly well the work of an administrator or manager at any level, regardless of whether he is the president of a big corporation, the top executive of a union, or the head of a government agency. They represent what a top management official is concerned with, but, on the other hand, a straw boss at the lowest supervisory level, with only four or five workers and a relatively small number of simple tasks to perform, is concerned to some degree with similar elements. Of course there is a vast difference in scope and importance between the two, but fundamentally these areas describe the processes that take place in the management of an enterprise. These same five groups of activity are present in varying degrees in all the intermediate levels of management.

Although each of the five processes must be performed, they do not necessarily take place separately; there is much overlapping. An executive may be planning a reorganization of his department to secure better control; he can give directions and instructions to achieve better coordination. A careful checkup on any of these activities may require additional planning or replanning of various aspects. An executive does not set aside two hours on Tuesday to do his coordinating for the week. He uses these processes as the mechanic uses tools: when they are needed and by selecting the proper one for the task at hand.

THE MANAGEMENT CYCLE

Although each of these five primary processes are used whenever needed, there is a certain phasing or sequence in their use. Certainly no one should plunge into an important activity without first thinking through what is needed. Planning is involved, and firm decisions have to be made. When looking for a solution to a problem, either immediate or foreseen, the manager starts to plan the appropriate action. This is the first phase.

Often the situation requires immediate action. The executive then has to have his subordinate employees carry out the decision. Several things are required to accomplish this second phase of securing effective executive action. There must be an efficient organization through which the desired results can be effected. Directions and instructions must be furnished to everyone concerned. The various aspects of the action must be coordinated so the whole operation will proceed harmoniously. If the plan is for the future, the same actions must be taken when and if the expected situation occurs.

Finally, there must be real assurance that the actions produced the results desired. This means exercising sufficient control over the operation to prevent errors during the procedures and to ensure a successful conclusion. Sometimes plans do not work out exactly as contemplated. Important facts may have been missing or some of the information incorrect. The executive may not have been in top form when he made the decision. However, when he sees the plan in action and finds certain changes are desirable, he has additional facts to work with and can think through and replan for more effective action. Thus, the cycle of planning, executive action, and control starts over. The three phases are shown in diagrammatic form in Figure 1.

The human element is shown as being central to all the management processes. Even though personnel management is not the theme of this book, it is necessary to remember that the executive should constantly be aware of the importance of his relations with the other people in the enterprise. Because a manager gets results through the efforts of other people, he is dependent upon them for his success. In his book, *The Practice of Management*,[6] Peter F. Drucker states that one of the most important functions of an executive is to review the performance of his subordinate managers and supervisors to help them effectively in their own self-development. And, it has been well said that you cannot teach an old dog new tricks unless you know more than the dog.

These relationships can be illustrated in many ways. Table 1 presents another approach that may help clarify the operation of the cycle. It combines the five primary management processes defined earlier into these three phases. The purpose of combining them is to stress that planning, organizing, directing, coordinating, and controlling usually take place in some

---

[6] Peter F. Drucker, *The Practice of Management*, Harper and Brothers, New York, 1954.

sequence and are thus repeated in a cyclical manner. The way
these aspects of a manager's work are carried out will be described more fully later.

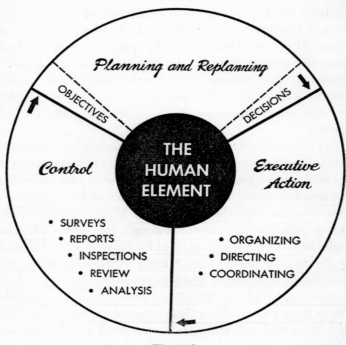

Figure 1

MANAGEMENT FROM SUPERIORS

Up to this point, the discussion has described in broad terms
how one goes about managing a job. But, management is not
only what you *do* in relation to the work and workers under
your direction; it is also what you *receive* from higher levels
of the organization. People may think the president of a cor-

ANALYSIS			ACTION		APPRAISAL
Evaluation of the situation	*Immediate cause*	*Basic cause*	*Stimulus to change*	*Provision of means*	*Evaluation of results*
Factual analysis of problem areas in relation to goals. The factors of quality and quantity of product or services are defined in the statement of purpose. Most actual problems affecting the efficient accomplishment of the objectives can be resolved on a cost basis, such as: 1. High costs of operations 2. High overhead 3. Wastes, errors, rejects, and spoilage of materials. Work situations are continuously changing, so evaluations should be frequent and thorough.	Exploration of immediate cause of inefficient productivity (or high costs) and identification of reasons, such as: 1. Poor organization 2. Poor communication 3. Low morale 4. High turnover 5. Absenteeism 6. Lack of job skills 7. Poor methods 8. Bad layout Action should be taken immediately to eliminate the causes of inefficient operation *but the* analysis should not be stopped until the *basic* cause has been identified and corrective action taken to prevent future trouble.	Recognition that each of the immediate causes of problems stem from the failure of some *person,* such as: 1. To plan adequately 2. To act effectively This is an area of executive or supervisory responsibility that can be strengthened but, because of human fallibility, never reaches perfection.	Creation of a climate conducive to improvement, a willingness to cooperate in reducing the basic cause of management problems. The following features are essential to such a climate: 1. The stimulus must emanate from the top 2. Personal encouragement and assistance from superior officials are necessary 3. Participation by employee or supervisory groups should be encouraged 4. The need for improvement must be recognized.	Improvement of management competence at all levels by developing the ability of all employees to perform assigned duties effectively. This includes: 1. Development of executives 2. Supervisor training 3. Orientation 4. Job skills training These items utilize such techniques as: self-development special assignment coaching on the job participation in conferences and work meetings, informal training, and in trade or professional associations As indicated in column 2, corrective action must be taken promptly to reduce immediate causes of problems. Prevention of future difficulties comes through the means utilized to remove the basic cause.	Appraisal of the action taken. The inquiry is in two phases: 1. Did the action eliminate or reduce are causes of the trouble? 2. Is the total program for management improvement solving the fundamental operating problems described in column 1? When evaluation shows the results have not been wholly satisfactory, further analysis is needed; a new problem situation has arisen. Identification of causes and provision for corrective and preventive actions carries the process through the original cycle again.

TABLE 1. Creative Problem Solving

poration is the supreme authority in that organization, but even he is subject to plans, policies, procedures, and decisions from the board of directors. The directors, in turn, are subject to management by the stockholders, by government agencies, and, sometimes, even by the public.

In your day-to-day work, then, you are being "managed" in the sense that you receive orders, directions, and instructions; policy and procedural statements; rules and regulations; work standards, specifications and deadlines; or quotas, ceilings, and fund limitations. Every one of these has an impact because they tell you what to do and restrict your freedom to operate as you please. It is not surprising, therefore, that executives sometimes resent and even resist these limitations to their jobs and their initiative to operate as they wish.

Such attitudes are usually harmful. They disclose ignorance of the nature of management, particularly with respect to how authority and responsibility are delegated downward.[7] They smack of insubordination or at least lack of loyalty and coopera- tion. They indicate failure to understand the need for decisions at higher levels and for direction and control of operations. Persons who feel this way often fail to discharge their own management responsibilities adequately because they do not understand what the management processes really are.

Actually, few people like change unless they initiate it them- selves. It is understandable that executives working under high pressure may be momentarily disturbed by a manage- ment directive making a change mandatory. The wise individ- ual conceals such annoyance and assumes there is a good reason for the decision, based on the judgment of persons higher in the organization than himself who have a broader

---

[7] Some writers contend that, although authority may be delegated, re- sponsibility is always retained. This can be defended as a theory, but in practice bosses continue to give responsibility to their subordinates.

view of the total situation. Realizing people are upset by changes, it is becoming common management practice to set forth the reasons for any change, either before or at the time of the announcement or shortly thereafter. If, by inadvertence, a supervisor receives an order for a major change without an explanation for it, he should find out what the reasons really are.

DEVELOPMENT OF COMPETENCE TO MANAGE

Management must be learned through practice

Experience is the most important element in becoming a competent manager. Practical arts, such as management, cannot be learned from books, lectures, seminars, conferences, or off-the-job training; they can only be learned by practice and experience.

Books and systematic study can, however, make the process of "learning by experience" more fruitful and effective. They can teach a person in management to be more reflective about his experience and to note and understand more clearly what is happening to him, and about him, in his work. They can also help him to systematize his experience, to perceive more clearly what is lacking, and to fill in the gaps.

Variations in aptitude for managing

There are some practical aspects of executive development that should be kept in mind. One of these is the normal variation between individuals in aptitude to manage. Although everyone can learn to manage well, each person possesses different characteristics and attributes that can hamper or facilitate development. The man with a bad temper, one he has not learned to curb, will be handicapped by it in making correct decisions in some cases. The individual who can readily see matters in their true relationships tends to build an efficient organization. Each person varies in habits, attributes, and feelings. Each has his own strengths and weaknesses. Because there are no perfect people, there are obviously no perfect managers.

One aspect of aptitude to manage merits special attention. This is the tendency of an executive to delegate, or not to delegate, authority to his subordinates. The second condition is more common. Many people hesitate to release any authority and insist that everything be brought to their attention. The opposite extreme where a manager tries to delegate everything, including his own responsibilities, to his employees is equally undesirable. The basic responsibility for results must be retained even though other obligations can be delegated to one's subordinates. Most successful managers delegate wisely, that is, the maximum extent without loss of control.

If it were possible to measure how much aptitude and experience two people had in the five processes of management, the result might look something like Figure 2.

Both of these diagrams represent normal people who are actually superior executives. Bill is better than average in planning and checking on his work and outstanding in his ability to give directions and coordinate activities. But he does not have the same competence in organizing his department, so he would not do well in a position where he was responsible for a basic overhaul of the organizational structure. He would do his best work in a stable unit where his strengths could be used to best advantage.

Jack, on the other hand, comes up with excellent plans, has his division well organized, and directs operations efficiently. He fails to give the same attention to inspections and standards and does not achieve smooth, uninterrupted work flow. Jack probably would not do well with a major assembly operation where he has to handle the flow of parts or one where quality of product was highly important.

Of course it is possible that both Bill and Jack may have more aptitude in these areas than they show, and with sufficient effort and training they might be able to remedy their deficiencies.

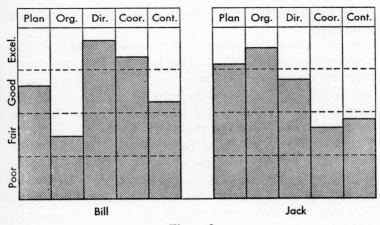

Figure 2

Appraisal of management performance

It is impossible to measure exactly how anyone would fit on such a scale, but it is possible to appraise an executive's performance against the requirements of the job and estimate fairly well how he is doing. When you know the directions in which you are managing most effectively, you can use these strengths to better advantage. When you discover what your weak spots are, you can take steps to strengthen them. Although anyone can develop his competence in any of the management processes, progress is slower and more difficult in areas where the person has less aptitude. Some persons fail to grow because they are not willing to make a strong effort or they become discouraged quickly.

Knowledge, skills, and attitudes

It does not take much research to show that most people in executive positions can improve their performance substantially. There are three main areas in which improvements may be possible.

Knowledge. Some persons lack an understanding of what modern management really is. They have had little opportunity to review the developments occurring in the last few decades, and they do not understand the principles on which management is based. Others are not informed about developments in their own line of work or the policies of their company.

Skills. Other persons may have read widely and kept informed theoretically about the doctrines of management but failed to develop or apply them in their daily work. Management competence is more than a question of exposure to knowledge. All professional training involves development of skills. Among the most important ones for the businessman are skill in decision-making, despite uncertainty and incomplete information, and skill in human relations and communication.

Attitudes. With some people the trouble is mainly one of attitude. They have feelings and prejudices that reduce their efficiency and preclude their development as superior executives. They lack motivation to change. While managers must give adequate attention to skills and knowledge, psychologists point out that emotions are the triggers setting off actions. People act in a certain way because of their interests, desires, fears, or dislikes. They behave, or misbehave, in response to their feelings. If this is even partially true, attitude may be the key to the direction, speed, and distance you will travel in improving your competence as a manager.

Regardless of how effective a person's attitude is, without knowledge as a basis on which to act, his performance as a manager is not likely to improve. It has been said that "What we are up on, we are not down on." Familiarity with the processes of management as a result of study, such as participating in a training program, often creates interest and provides the incentive to change. Practice of the techniques also may bring about motivation to improve. An appeal from someone on a higher level may arouse the desire to learn how to manage more competently. For most people, pride in superior accomplishment plus interest in their own growth provide the incentive needed.

SUMMARY

Not until the twentieth century did people begin to have a real understanding of what takes place when men manage an enterprise. Although knowledge is still incomplete and imperfect, it is certain that the five basic management processes described in this chapter are important aspects of successful accomplishment. Experience indicates that the actions often occur in a sequence or cycle. Observations of all sorts of enterprises show that persons with a great deal of responsibility use these managerial processes more than persons in lower levels of the organization. Even so, foremen and supervisors have some management responsibilities to discharge and need at least an elementary understanding of how to manage well. As they are promoted within the organization, their competence to manage must be further developed.

The ability to manage effectively can be learned. Although everyone progresses differently because of differences in understanding, degree of skill, attitude, and ability to assume a leadership role, those who understand the management processes progress faster and farther than those without this knowledge.

PART TWO

Planning and Making Sound Decisions

Because executives are responsible for managing the work assigned to them, they must plan carefully to keep all operations reasonably efficient and to achieve the objectives of the enterprise. Both analytical and creative thinking are needed to decide what is to be done, by whom, where, when, and, to some degree, how. Part Two describes the important process of planning, for both immediate and future situations.

2

Planning

Planning is usually regarded as thinking through the actions necessary to accomplish a purpose. It requires looking ahead to estimate future situations and needs, and judgment and discretion to determine the most effective actions. An important part of all work management, planning involves the selection of a company's objectives, policies, programs, procedures, schedules, and budgets from the various alternatives. Thus, planning results in decisions that affect the future course of an enterprise.

One company defines planning as thinking work through before it is performed. Another looks upon it as the thinking that precedes the actual performance of work. A third company finds that planning primarily involves intellectual faculties and thought processes because it requires imagination, foresight, and sound judgment. Thus, planning is used in such activities as identification and evaluation of business opportunities and hazards; determination of the course or objectives of a business, or a division of a business, to increase effectiveness or achieve profits; establishment of policies and the continuous seeking and finding of new and better ways of doing things. Thorough planning always includes determining the steps required to accomplish the goals after they are established.

PLANNING AS THINKING

Research under way at the University of Southern California by Dr. J. P. Guilford and his associates [1] is throwing new light on the planning process. This group is making substantial progress in studying the structure of the intellect and the various factors that are involved. Presently it appears that the main areas of intellectual activity are related as shown in the following diagram.

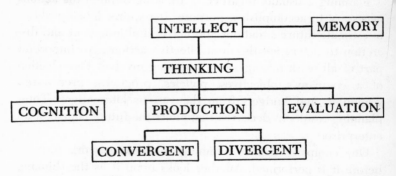

As the chart indicates, the memory function is considered to be separate from thinking, yet it is indispensable to all thinking because it enables us to recall from our mental storehouse the particular items needed for our thought processes. We cannot think in a mental vacuum. Although some things do not always come to mind when needed, Friedrich Nietzsche

[1] "A Revised Structure Of Intellect," Studies of Aptitudes of High-level Personnel, Reports from the Psychological Laboratory, No. 19, The University of Southern California, April, 1957.

pointed out long ago that the existence of forgetting has never been proved. Hypnosis and truth serums can be used to bring back experiences that apparently had become completely forgotten. It would seem then that recalling can be stimulated and that a better memory will result in better planning.

The thinking abilities fall into three major categories. One is cognition. It has to do with recognizing and becoming aware of things, events, or concepts. It is what is commonly called "learning" and includes discovering and comprehending what goes on. Another type of thinking, evaluation, concerns itself with making choices. It is the mental activity that results in decisions about accuracy, feasibility, suitability, goodness, and the like. It is often called judicial thinking because it requires the use of judgment. The third type, production thinking, uses pertinent information to secure certain results. It seeks to find solutions to problems and answers to questions. It is the kind of thinking that managers engage in many times daily. The study shows that productive thinking can take place in two different ways. The convergent type is what is often called logical or analytical thinking. This type of thinking assumes that there is one right answer and seeks to find it. Sometimes it accepts the first answer that appears when a better one might have been found. Divergent thinking, on the other hand, reaches out, searches, and explores many channels for possible solutions. It is the creative type of thinking that is receiving so much attention in many businesses. It looks for new, unusual, unique, and improved ways to conduct an enterprise. As will be seen, planning makes use of all of these intellectual powers.

PLANNING AS PROBLEM SOLVING

Many people who have studied the planning process used in work management consider it as thinking through, studying, or analyzing work situations. These situations almost always involve a problem, either anticipated or unforeseen.

The most effective planning visualizes problems that may arise, considers them, and determines what should be done. In other words, good management does not wait until the situation becomes critical to make a decision.

The problems faced in job planning take many forms: how to organize a unit; what equipment is needed; how much space; what kinds of abilities are there in the work force; how much responsibility should be delegated; how much production can be reasonably expected; or any one of a thousand similar things. Management plans its financing, public relations, methods of control, and coordination. When a decision is reached, it is written down and becomes the actual plan.

Decisions about job problems can also take several forms. For example:

1. Policy—when you decide about what is to be done in a given situation, you are establishing the policy to be followed in your unit.

2. Procedure—when you make up your mind about how the job is to be done, you are setting up an operating procedure to be followed.

3. Organization—when you decide where in your unit the various specalized tasks are to be grouped and related for effective action, you are establishing an organizational pattern.

These three steps give the clue to an important principle: planning runs through every aspect of work management from start to finish, day in and day out.

MAJOR ASPECTS OF PLANNING

An analysis of planning discloses five important aspects of the process.

Formulating the objective

In business, planning starts with an assumption that certain products can be made or services rendered at a profit. The basic objective is set by this assumption. Probably most people think of E. I. Du Pont de Neymours & Co. as a huge corporation primarily designed to make profits for its stockholders. Certainly this is an obvious and legitimate goal; the company could not operate at a loss for long without danger of bankruptcy. Yet in its advertising, the Du Pont slogan, "Better things for better living through chemistry," sets a different objective. In its factories, a special purpose is the manufacture of unusual synthetics. Each department in the Delaware plants also has clearly defined its own goals; workers in each shop or segment know exactly what is to be accomplished, down to the individual employee.

There are objectives to be achieved at every level in all organizations. How they are attained depends upon the effectiveness of the planning. More accurately, the efficiency at the operating level depends on how well the managers handled the planning function. Unless managers fully understand what results are expected of them, they cannot plan their work effectively.

Estimating the situation

After an objective has been identified and defined, the planning process starts by analyzing the situation as it exists or as it is foreseen. Here the planner asks himself (and others), "What are the pertinent facts that bear on this situation? What assumptions can we safely make? Where can I get the information I need? Who can help me? What questions should I ask?" The answers to questions like these provide grist for the thinking mill. Planning is sound only to the extent that the answers are sound.

At this point the planner sometimes fails to do an adequate job because he tends to push ahead too rapidly, to avoid the laborious task of finding information to help plan more soundly, or to accept the first solution that comes to mind. Obviously you can never get all the facts about a situation, nor should you want to. It is important, however, to secure enough information to understand clearly what is involved. If you are dealing with an existing situation, you can go to the spot and observe what the conditions are. It is different, however, if you are making a plan to fit a contingency. In this case, you have to make a number of assumptions about what might happen.

It is often difficult to secure the information needed. Sometimes it just does not exist, or extensive research is necessary to find it. Other persons may have part of the information you need, and you should enlist their cooperation. However, what appears to be fact may later turn out to be incorrect. Much of what you find will have little or no bearing on the real problem. So you probe into your own experiences, review available records, question others, read pertinent books or articles, or experiment, all in the hope of accumulating enough relevant information to decide the best way to achieve the objective.

Interpreting the facts

At this point, the situation is comparable to a table covered with pieces from a jigsaw puzzle. Some are face down and therefore are meaningless; others, by color or design, show they are parts of a picture. There may be pieces from more than one puzzle, and, to make it more difficult, you do not know if all you need are there. So you must sort them out to find out how they fit together and to see if they make a complete picture or if key pieces are still missing.

In planning, it always helps to get the facts out where you can see what you have to work with. Many persons use 3×5 cards with a fact recorded on each and shuffle them around to help bring out relationships. Others use charts to put the various items in some kind of pattern. Some people try to carry out this part of the planning process mentally. Unfortunately, there is a limit to the amount of material anyone can consciously keep in mind. Unless the situation is relatively simple, it is advisable to write down all of the facts so none are overlooked.

The more you study the items, the more clearly you see how they fit together. There are usually two main sets of relationships. One has to do with cause and effect. "What caused this to happen? What was the effect of that action? How could we bring such a condition about?" This kind of thinking often brings facts into even clearer relationships and begins to show the real situation. The other set of relationships has to do with time sequence. "Which event takes place first? Should it come first? Is there a chain of actions timewise? Are they in the right order?" Putting facts in proper sequence may show additional relationships and help further clarify the situation.

This kind of interpretation discloses areas where more facts are needed and weeds out items that do not seem pertinent. However, the best planners do not discard these apparently useless bits of information completely because later they may turn out to have real significance. Sometimes startling discoveries are made from pieces that had little relationship to the situation at first glance. Eventually a clear picture will form, but, until it *is* clear, the planning process is incomplete.

Drawing ~~tentative conclusions~~

Through study and analysis of the situation, you naturally get ideas of what could be done to bring about the condition you want. Several possible courses of action might come to mind. These ideas should not be allowed to escape because they may contain the answer you need. If you do not write them down immediately, nine times out of ten something puts them out of your mind, and they are lost forever. The more the picture clears, the more valid your ideas become. Toward the end of the analysis stage, you should have a number of tentative or alternate possibilities, any one, or combination, of which may contain the best course of action.

At this point you can draw on your imagination, and, by divergent thinking, find new and more effective possibilities. Creative problem-solving is recognized by business, industry, government, and educational institutions as a sound and rewarding effort. Many large corporations believe so thoroughly in the value of creative techniques that they teach them to the beginning scientific and engineering employees. General Electric Co. stated that this training increased the number of *usable* ideas from its beginners by 300 per cent.

Some people hesitate to plan comprehensively because they think they lack the vision, resourcefulness, and imagination necessary to do so. Such qualities are certainly helpful in discovering new and more effective solutions. Lack of vision can be a great handicap. One of the best ways to develop it, however, is to do exactly what is advocated in this chapter. Every intelligent person has the ability to imagine, and imagination can be stimulated. You may wish to read *Applied Imagination* [2]

[2] Alex Osborn, *Applied Imagination,* Charles Scribner's Sons, New York, 1957 (Revised in January, 1958).

by Alex Osborn to learn what you can do to develop your creative powers. In any event, the only way to increase your ability to plan well and to solve business problems soundly is constant practice.

Deciding on the final plan

The more divergent thought used in your search for possible solutions, the greater variety of ideas you have to choose from. Because there is a choice, you must use evaluative thinking— your judgment. This shift in types of thinking is natural. Creative and judicial thinking should always be used alternatively not concurrently. When the imagination is being used, any attempt to evaluate ideas puts a damper on originality and slows down the flow of new ideas. Later, when all the suggestions have been made, judgment is necessary to choose between them.

So, in this final stage, the question is which of several possible courses of action is the best one. Decisions of this kind are not always easy to make, and because they have far-reaching effects, they must be sound decisions. The next chapter is devoted to the subject of making management decisions.

THE NATURE OF PLANS

Possibly the most common use of the word "plan" is in connection with building. No architect, or even a competent carpenter, would think of starting a building without a plan. First, the design and use (its purpose or objective) must be determined. Then, there must be a complete and detailed estimate of the situation which requires marshaling of the technical know-how and experience of many people. Decisions have to be made about materials, space, equipment, financing, the construction work force, and similar matters.

Eventually all these data are brought together in "the plans." First is a set of blueprints that show exactly the kind of a structure to be built. It is the basic guide used by the architect, carpenters, masons, plumbers, electricians, painters, and inspectors. The blueprints tell *what* is to be done in this particular situation.

Blueprints do not indicate *how* the work is to be performed, so the specifications are added. The workmen are given step-by-step instructions on each operation: how the footings are to be poured, what grades of materials are to be used, how the insulation is to be installed, and how the interior is to be finished. The blueprints and specifications give all the information needed to complete the building.

Types of Plans

The illustration above could apply either to a structure that is to be built right now or one planned for construction later. All management planning can be similarly classified as either short- or long-range planning.

The former is used in a situation or problem that needs immediate attention. Action is necessary to correct an existing difficulty or to make a change desired by superior authority. Sometimes there is little time available before the action must be taken, so planning must be done quickly. If word is received at 1:30 P.M. that a progress report on Work Order 74392 must be in the boss's office by 2 P.M., things must happen with dispatch. Yet some plans must be made so the correct facts are secured and sent before the deadline. The responsible supervisor estimates the situation, quickly reviews what is known about the order, and decides who is to do what. Should he go to the plant himself, send someone, or telephone? Can he get the necessary information from production planning? Should the information be dictated to the boss's secretary or typed and delivered directly to the boss? Should the supervisor deliver it personally in case further questions arise? Although this is a typical situation, in other instances considerably more time is available before action must be taken, providing an opportunity for more careful planning.

Much planning is designed to give guidance on what to do if or when a specified situation arises in the future. Good managers look ahead in order to be prepared for all eventualities. Thus, there are plans for employee retirement, for retirement of bond issues, for fire emergencies, or for machine tool breakdown. The objective may be presently unattainable, such as interstellar travel or an unbreakable code, but planning can go on working toward the final goal. It took years of planning to produce the Salk vaccine for polio and to make the atomic bomb. American business is looking far into the future in much of its planning; neither the dial telephone nor color television was developed overnight.

Flexibility

In long-range planning, it is particularly necessary to provide for change. As more information is available even the objective itself may change. Many times it is impossible to find out everything necessary to make firm decisions, so a tentative plan has to be made, subject to modification.

If all conditions cannot be foreseen, it may be wise to prepare alternate plans. A business that is outgrowing its present quarters must look ahead to decide what its course of action is to be. One solution may be to purchase additional land and erect new buildings. Another may be to build additions to the present structures. A third may be to move the entire activity to a new location. Each of these possibilities could be worked out in considerable detail so a higher authority is able to decide which plan is most feasible. Or all of them could be held in abeyance until action is necessary and final determination made in light of conditions existing then.

PLANNING AS FORECASTING

Because long-range planning is so important to good management, it is necessarily a prominent part of an executive's job. Unless a manager can look ahead and predict the future of his operations with some accuracy, he will constantly be caught unprepared. Most successful men have the ability to forecast future trends and events and to make advance plans to meet contingencies. Some people are so successful in this respect they are credited with special gifts or even subtle powers of divination.

It is possible an individual will occasionally make a lucky guess about the future, but the chances that guessing will hit upon the correct answer are unfavorable because there are too many factors involved. The man who bases his job planning on intuition is taking long chances indeed, not only with his own reputation but also with the job stability of all those under his direction. Responsible officials have to do better than that.

Long-range planning is inherent in any continuing enterprise. This forecasting cannot be a hit-or-miss affair because too much is at stake. Plans must be based upon every bit of information and trend that is available. All pertinent data are accumulated, past experience recalled, expert advice obtained, and complicated statistical methods utilized to make certain the preview is as accurate as humanly possible.

After such exhaustive study, some assumptions must be made at the highest level before the action, or actions, to be taken can be decided upon. Normally there are alternatives to be considered. *If* the productive capacity of the steel industry reaches 120 per cent of the past five–year average in the next five years, it will be possible to supply 15,000 automobiles per week. However, *if* the ore situation reduces in productive capacity, the assumption is that only 5,000 such items can be supplied.

At the January, 1956, General Management Conference of the American Management Association in San Francisco Charles B. Thornton, Chairman of Board and President of Litton Industries, Inc., pointed out that even though you cannot foresee the future conditions you may face with complete certainty, you can predict most of the possible alternative conditions that may materialize with reasonable accuracy. You can provide for each of these contingencies to a satisfactory degree. When courses of action have been decided upon, they are passed down to lower levels for further planning by those who have the responsibility for carrying out the broad over-all plans.

Another prominent executive pointed out that under average operating conditions he could do very little to affect the current results of those conditions because the ongoing momentum of the organization was too great. However, he felt he could do a great deal to influence the results expected in five or ten years.

This illustrates the importance of the time element. One company took more than two years to secure a five–year sales forecast on a company-wide basis. Yet obviously sales and profit projections must be made in order to develop final plans for new products, market development, facilities, or capital requirements.

Within any organizational segment of a business or institution, similar, but necessarily more limited, forecasting is required. Although attention must be focused on the current situation, it is also necessary to look ahead at times to be sure future operations will be efficient. This is the only way to be prepared for eventualities. Not all future events can be forecasted, but it is surprising how many can be predicted. The more you are forewarned of changes, the better prepared you are to meet them.

It is difficult to describe exactly how such planning takes place because there are many equally valid approaches and stimulators. However, it is possible to recognize the aspects of forecasting that usually appear somewhere in the process and the order in which they most frequently occur.

Securing advance information

Plans made by higher authorities are one of the logical sources from which forecasting stems. Few enterprises can continue to operate efficiently without guidance from above. Many times it is in the form of new or modified plans based on facts or assumptions agreed to by top management.

Such plans are usually general and affect broad areas of the organization. Plans established by the board of directors may change the purpose of an entire department or influence operations in every subordinate plant. These effects are necessarily reflected even at the lowest organizational level.

Because your own operations can be seriously affected by higher level planning, it is to your advantage to find out the nature of such changes as early as possible. The sooner you ascertain the direction and extent of your involvement, the more time you have to plan for the change.

Even before new plans are ready for issuance in final form, their nature is often apparent. Although all of the details may not be settled, the general direction of the change will be known. This type of advance information will be helpful to you. Sometimes you hear of such proposals through rumors, but about the only place you can secure confirmation is from your own boss. Even he may not be fully informed but he may appreciate being tipped off so he can find out what is contemplated.

In this case, a close job relationship with your superior pays off. If he respects your judgment and discretion, he will take you into his confidence and, by working together, you can be adequately prepared to put the new plan into operation. Because time is of major importance in the development of operating plans, you may be able to devise far more effective ways to make the change than if you learned about it later. The additional time provides an opportunity for more consultation with your subordinates so obstacles can be identified and removed. This, in turn, results in a smoother transition and a more efficient final operation.

Studying trends

Any manager who consistently studies his operation will note, from time to time, that conditions are changing. Costs are rising. Production is increasing. Labor turnover is decreasing. Accidents are more frequent. Machine down time is on the rise. Even in a stable organization, both men and machines are getting older. Some of these trends may not be significant, but others may have a great deal of meaning.

Many supervisors keep cumulative records of these changes. The data can be compared over a period of time to indicate the development of any trends. Other supervisors find charts show the changes more plainly. A trial of these visual devices over a few weeks or months will indicate the ones most useful and desirable for you. In general, the more simple they are, the better because they are usually easier to maintain and interpret. If it is too much trouble to keep them up-to-date or if mistakes occur in the recording, the charts are useless. You may want to consult someone in the organization to help you plan the most helpful charts.

It is not sufficient to merely secure and record information about your work. Significant trends must be identified and studied. In fact, most changes must be studied to determine whether they are significant. Study means asking pertinent questions and getting the answers. "What is the reason for this change? What should I do about it? Is it due to circumstances beyond my control? Does it represent a pattern that will be repeated? What effect will it have on operations? If it continues, what should I do about it? When? Is the rate of change increasing or decreasing? Will it reach a peak? When? Will it diminish or continue? Why?" It is not easy to find the answers to such questions but good planners try to do so.

Reviewing past experiences

The quality of forecasting depends upon the wisdom used in planning. A wise person profits from experience. Long-range planning should apply the lessons learned from the previous experiences of the planner and his associates. This is so obvious it is trite. Yet this resource is not always used as effectively as it might be.

No situation is completely new; many aspects will resemble other situations faced before. The first problem, then, is to analyze the contemplated change and identify the aspects that parallel previously encountered conditions. The more closely you study a proposal, the more clearly you perceive the parts where experience already found a feasible answer. The solution that worked well before can be applied again to the extent that the two situations are alike.

This is not to say you should blindly follow precedent. There may be better ways to get the result; we do make progress. However, by drawing parallels, you have a useful approach to planning: a tentative answer that can be modified. An answer that may work is far better than no answer at all.

In your study of the trends and information, you should continue to ask questions. "Does this condition resemble anything I have faced before? In what ways? How is it different? What solutions worked in previous cases? Would the same ones work here? Has Tom, Dick, or Harry ever faced a similar problem? Could they help formulate this part of the plan? What have other divisions done in cases like this?"

If, as Shakespeare put it, "What's past is prologue," you can call upon the past to help you plan tomorrow's activities. Your experience and that of others form a vast reservoir from which to draw ideas. Consciously probing into this pool of experience contributes to better forecasting and long-range planning.

Making assumptions

At what point in planning should assumptions be made? In many cases, it will be early in the process. It is necessary to assume the proposed change will actually occur as described; the trend will continue, diminish, or reverse; facilities can be provided; technical know-how will be available; or there will be no serious disturbance to the work force.

Questions on points similar to these will arise throughout the planning. If you could be absolutely certain of the answers, there would be no need to make assumptions. Because you cannot be sure, you have to seek a tentative answer, based upon all the facts available but involving the risk that it may not be perfect. All future planning involves such risks because you never can have all the facts in advance. The important thing is to think through the situation carefully, recognize the risks, and make assumptions with a full knowledge of what is involved.

At this point many managers fall down because they are unwilling or afraid to take the risk. They do not understand that it is part of their jobs, and that they must have the courage of their convictions. Of course, some of the assumptions may be false, but this does not mean they should not be made. Predictions are seldom completely wrong. Normally, it is merely necessary to recognize the changed situation and modify plans to fit it.

Preparing operational plans

Up to this point the thinking process that precedes the formulation of a definite plan of action has been discussed. Now it is possible to crystallize this thinking. The best way is to put it on paper, spelling out simply and clearly what is to be done if and when the expected situation actually occurs.

At operational levels, such plans usually are rather brief. They identify the situation so no one will be confused as to what it is. They state what is to be done and who will do it. They may prescribe how certain operations should be handled, but much of the method may be left up to the subordinates. The objective is to clarify the proposed actions to each unit and each person involved understands what is expected. The plan then serves as an explicit guide to the work force when it is needed.

If the organization is large or the plan contains complicated instructions, more detail is required. There may be a breakdown with separate plans for different segments. Charts often help to portray relationships, time sequences, work flow, or changes in organizational structure.

It is desirable to have persons who will be affected by possible changes participate in the preparation of the plan. This permits a broader base of experiences and facilitates understanding and acceptance of the plan. The more completely you can involve the people you have to work with, in the actual drafting of the plan, the more assurance you have of its successful application. Persons who take part in preparing a plan are likely to do their best to make it work.

Although most long-range plans will not be put into effect unless the anticipated situation actually arises, there are instances where the event is certain to happen. In these cases it is appropriate to phase the plan, that is, to space the preparatory actions over the time available so everyone is ready when the change occurs. Thus, even though the change may not happen for a considerable time, preliminary steps can be initiated immediately to establish a firm foundation for the transition. Requisitions can be prepared for equipment or materials. Steps can be taken to secure the additional employees who will be needed. Some training can be given to prepare the work force. New record systems can be devised. The time interval is used to good advantage by putting such step-by-step procedures into the plan.

CHECKING THE PLANS

It is common experience to find that, no matter how carefully plans were made, the result does not exactly meet expectations. Possibly all of the facts were not available, some of the items misunderstood, or part of the data incorrect.

To guard against major errors in plans, it is desirable to review them for feasibility. The more people who can check over the plans, the better. Many of the comments will not be helpful, but it is surprising how many sound suggestions will be made. This type of review brings additional experience and background to bear on the situation and helps to find the bugs in the plan before it goes into operation.

Another device that is often used is to set up a trial run of the plan. This is not always possible, but, when it can be done, it points out places where the planning was faulty. To be most helpful, the trial should be staged to resemble the actual situation as closely as possible. Those who participate must clearly understand their parts, which means some training is necessary. Sometimes it is possible to set up a simulated work situation, letting one desk represent an entire operation. This type of tryout is helpful if routing of papers or parts is important. The comments of participants should be noted during the trial and studied later for possible improvements in the plan.

If errors, inconsistencies, or rough spots are found, replanning is necessary to eliminate the trouble. It is far better to take the time to discover inadequacies and correct them in advance than to wait until the plan is put into execution to find the mistakes.

SECURING APPROVAL

Many plans made in day-to-day operations require the approval of a higher authority before they can be put into effect. This comes about if the plan affects other work areas, requires expenditures you are not authorized to make, or involves a change in established policy or procedures.

Securing such approval is often a matter that, in itself, requires some planning. It is seldom sufficient to get passive acceptance from a superior. Complete understanding, full agreement, and enthusiastic support are desirable to ensure the successful operation of the plan.

In the first place, the wise planner will check and recheck his proposal to be certain he has eliminated the bugs. Then, he will want to make sure the format of the material is attractively presented, complete, and comprehended easily. Presumably, he asked for all of the help he could secure from persons who will be affected by the plan and has their support.

Probably he laid the groundwork for approval by discussing the idea informally with his chief during various stages of the planning. One good way to get plans accepted is to keep your superior informed and get approval as you go along. Most bosses shy away from plans sprung on them all at once.

When you are ready to put a plan into finished form, you may wish to consider a method that others found useful.

1. Open with a brief statement of the plan.

2. Follow with a direct assertion of the anticipated gains, that is, what the plan will accomplish in terms of savings, increased production, or improved employee relations.

3. Present the changes and innovations necessary to accomplish the result, step by step, using sketches, charts, tables, or photographs.

4. Answer the question of cost that is always in the reviewer's mind. If necessary, quote prices or at least give honest estimates.

5. Conclude with a brief restatement of the anticipated gains.

The pattern suggested above represents good common sense because it answers the basic questions that arise in one's mind in their normal order. It helps the busy executive appraise the proposal without having to ask for essential facts. Because executives are busy, you should time the presentation so the boss is sufficiently free from interruptions to give his full attention. Trying to secure acceptance when he is under pressure or harassed by other problems only invites failure. The day of the week and the time of the day are significant in the work habits of the individual. The axiom here is know your man. Good judgment in the character and timing of the approach often goes a long way in securing acceptance and approval.

SUMMARY

This chapter has presented what is involved in the planning process, for long- and short-range goals. In both cases there is a marked trend toward divergent or creative techniques in planning to solve problems, followed by evaluative thinking or judgment to determine which of the ideas or possible solutions has greatest value. Forecasting or predicting what actions might be necessary in the future is one of the most important aspects of planning even though it involves a certain amount of risk. Competent managers recognize this as a hazard inherent to their positions and accept it because they know being prepared for eventualities is one of the major benefits of planning. Finally, consideration was given to the matter of securing approval of operational plans when necessary.

3

Making Sound Decisions

Reference was made to the cyclical nature of the management processes in the first chapter. The chart on page 14 indicates that planning is based on an established purpose or goal and results in a decision on what is to be done. A growing number of students of management believe decision-making is the most important aspect of planning because it sets the course of action. In any event, it is significant enough to merit additional attention at this point.

ARRIVING AT CONCLUSIONS

Among the important responsibilities you face as a supervisor, one that comes up day after day, is the need to determine what action you or someone else should take. Sometimes these occasions come from above; more often they arise as questions from employees. Many times you become aware of them yourself. Regardless of where they originate, you have to face them and try to find the answers. More specifically, consider the following:

Do you always find it easy to give the *right* answer?
Do you always *have* the right answer?

47

Do you sometimes blunder and give the *wrong* answer?

Isn't everyone *embarrassed* occasionally in these respects?

Most people would admit that the answers to questions like these leave them a little uneasy. Yet the ability to make up his mind is one of the fundamental attributes that any responsible manager must possess. To a major degree, his efficiency as a manager depends upon his being able to make decisions when they are needed. Unless answers are forthcoming, your boss has no way of knowing what you are going to do. More important, unless subordinates get decisions on their difficulties, questions, and problems, it will be impossible for them to know what to do. Unguided action can lead to drastic results.

UNDERSTANDING THE TERMS

First, it is important to understand the terms. It was pointed out earlier that a manager is responsible for solving job problems of many kinds. Getting answers to questions was also mentioned. Is there any difference between the two?

Many of the questions asked in the course of the day are about matters of little consequence. They require only yes or no answers, ones that can be given almost without thinking. Such questions seldom cause much trouble. They have been called tactical decisions. However, all too frequently questions are asked that cannot be answered so easily. They pose problems that require careful thought before a decision can be made. Because of their impact upon the success or failure of a major aspect of the enterprise, they might be considered strategic matters demanding full attention. In either event, whether you merely answer a question for an employee or find a solution to a job problem, you have made a decision.

Actually what happens is probably something like this:

1. you become aware of a problem;
2. when you solve it, you have made a decision; and
3. then you can give the answer.

Whether it is called "answering questions," "solving problems," or "making decisions," it is all part of the same process because you make up your mind about a course of action.[1]

However, questions are not necessarily less important than problems. A questioning mind is essential in the most effective planning because a closed mind actually inhibits thought. Many authorities point out the importance of asking the right questions in the first place. The correct course of action is determined by such incisive questioning.

In the previous chapters it was indicated that decisions come as a result of thinking through a situation, a planning process. This is true, but it is necessary to remember that planning and decision-making occur in stages. You think about your objective or purpose and decide specifically what it is to be. You plan your organization to carry out the purpose and determine the best structural arrangement to serve your purpose. You plan courses of action and make up your mind about how to proceed. You analyze the situation to decide what controls you need. In other words, planning and decision-making alternate throughout the entire management cycle.

TWO WAYS OF FINDING ANSWERS

There are two common ways of making decisions, the spontaneous method and the planned method.

Everyone has met and worked with people who have all the answers; they start to tell you what to do before you can finish

---

[1] In this chapter the discussion is focused upon determining the best course of action. Other types of decisions might be considered, such as recognition, understanding, or enterprise, but in the final analysis any decision, even in these areas, affects what you or your associates will do.

stating the problem. What do you think is happening when a person gives these quick answers? Probably one, or more, of the following occurs:

He may be jumping to a conclusion without sufficient facts.
He may have a fixed opinion on the subject and thus not listen carefully.
He may be deciding on the way he feels more than on the way he thinks.

BUT

He could be fully acquainted with the situation and in a position to give a sound answer.

There are two quite different implications here. One is that the man is using snap judgment or intuition in making his decision, giving the first answer that comes into his mind and trusting to luck that he will be right. The other is that he really does base his decision on good judgment because his experience has included similar situations, and, as soon as he has assured himself what the conditions really are, he can give an answer that will work. Thus, even though it takes but a few moments, he does make a quick analysis and bases his decision on sound judgment. In this case, the man is really not making a hasty decision at all. He is planning his reply.

The only intelligent way to make a decision is by sufficient thinking through and planning to arrive at a sound solution. Many people have studied this matter of problem-solving. Most of them have come up with about the same ideas: The process of making a decision is not always as complex or difficult as it sometimes appears. In fact, it consists of steps that you would naturally take anyway. It may help to review them, however, to avoid the pitfalls that are sometimes encountered in trying to find the answers to difficult questions.

THE DECISION-MAKING PROCESS

The necessity for a decision is often considered as the difference between the way you want conditions and the way you find them. You want requisitions to be processed within forty-eight hours but find it is taking three days in many cases. You want your employees to work steadily and willingly but find a few who are unwilling to cooperate. You want warehouse items stacked safely but find some piles are leaning dangerously. In each of these instances, you become dissatisfied with existing conditions. In fact, dissatisfaction is usually the starting point for situations where a decision is required. Similar conditions constantly arise. What should be done about them?

One solution is to do nothing. Too frequently, under pressure of other duties, managers choose to ignore the matter or to postpone giving it attention, which amounts to the same thing. The inclination to avoid a troublesome condition is understandable; finding good answers is not always easy, and, unless time has been planned carefully, there may be little opportunity to think through the circumstances and make a sound decision. However, management men cannot put off these matters indefinitely. Sooner or later an answer must be forthcoming. There is a logical way to go about problem-solving. It involves the planning steps discussed previously. To bring the whole picture into proper perspective, here is a brief review of what goes on prior to making the decision and a more complete discussion of the final step.

Stating the problem clearly

Before you can make headway in planning, you must get a clear view of the situation you face. When trouble arises, you say you have a problem; but if someone asks, "Just what is your problem?" it is often difficult to put it into words. Yet, if you cannot state the situation clearly, it is not going to be easy to know exactly what you want to accomplish. In this sense, defining the problem is the same as setting up the objective. It lights up the target so you can see what you are shooting at: If your aim is steady, you can get close to the bull's eye without wasting shots or making a lot of misses. To use another illustration, the physician is not satisfied merely to treat the patient's symptoms. A fever can be reduced, but the trained mind is concerned with the cause of the fever. This is sometimes called seeking the critical factor or the condition that must be changed before anything else can be modified satisfactorily. In the same way, the competent supervisor thinks through all aspects of the difficulty to be certain he knows exactly what he is seeking. He may redefine his problem several times as he learns more about the situation. Foremen are often faced with what seems to be a problem of absenteeism. Yet as they study the situation, they find the *real* problem is a matter of transportation, housing, the World Series, epidemic influenza, or overwork. A high percentage of spoiled work may actually be a problem of forced machine speeds or the quality of material. In any case, once the problem is clearly defined, the answer is much easier to find.

Getting the pertinent facts

You cannot make much progress until you know the whole story. You may not be able to perceive the critical factor clearly until you find out more about the situation. So, after you have tentatively stated your problem, you should secure as much pertinent information as is possible in the time available. Sometimes this is very limited, as in an emergency. However, when a serious issue is involved, the wise executive will insist on sufficient time to investigate thoroughly. It is bad management to be maneuvered into a position where a decision must be made without sufficient facts. You should question every aspect of the situation: who, when, where, why, how, how many, how long, what happens? Naturally you will get many answers that do not apply, but you select those that do fit and go right ahead. A clear picture of the total situation is possible only as these details are available, and you can arrive at sound conclusions only when you see the picture clearly.

Analyzing the facts

It is easy to say, "Now you have the facts, go ahead and interpret them." But it is not always as easy as it sounds. School children are given all the necessary facts to solve a problem in mathematics, and it is easy for those who know how to solve it. Know-how is simply seeing the relationships that exist between facts. Some students can see at once which quantities are equal, where to multiply or where to divide, and what the results of adding or subtracting will be. These lucky ones find the assignment easy, but those who fail to see the relationships between the facts think the lesson is difficult. The same thing is true in all administrative or supervisory problems. You must ferret out these relationships by asking such questions as:

What caused this to happen?
What resulted from that action?
Did this happen before or after that?

By such queries, you begin to see causes and effects, time relationships, and personal connections. And, as with the jig-saw puzzle, when the pieces begin to fit together in a clear picture, the problem begins to make sense. In many kinds of problems the analysis not only seeks to find out these relationships but also includes a comparison of the accumulated facts to established standards, such as standards of conduct, performance, or production. By comparing the facts with these standards you are able to see new relationships and, thus, interpret the facts intelligently.

Identifying alternative solutions

As you think about the problem and analyze the facts, possible solutions will naturally occur to you. Suggestions may flash into your mind at unexpected times, especially if you ponder over the problem. As you talk the matter over with your employees, they may give you a clue. Any one of these ideas may be the answer, so you do not want to lose it. Furthermore, nearly every time you clinch a suggestion, you will think of other possible answers. This is a good way to encourage vision, initiative, and resourcefulness to function. Again, you should list every possibility for careful review later. The more ideas under consideration, the better your chances of improving the quality of the final decision.

Such situations lend themselves to creative thinking by both individuals and groups. Probably the most widely used group method is called brainstorming where a panel of eight to fifteen people use their imaginations to produce original ideas that might lead to one or more satisfactory solutions. During this period of ideation or divergent thinking, no judgment is permitted because it has been found that evaluation or criticism of the thoughts during the productive stage deters the flow of suggestions. Complete information about this method can be obtained from the Creative Education Foundation, Inc., or from the book, *Brainstorming*, by Charles H. Clarke.[2]

[2] Creative Education Foundation, Inc., 1614 Rand Bldg., Buffalo 3, N. Y.

Charles H. Clarke, *Brainstorming*, Doubleday & Company, Inc., New York, 1958.

Finding the best answer

The next step is fairly obvious. Selecting the best solution has been the goal from the start. But, again, there are some guides to help determine what really is the best answer. Many supervisors and executives apply three criteria at this point.

Suitability. The first question asked is, "Which of the possible answers will accomplish the results wanted?" You set up a definite goal when you defined your problem and redefined it later. You now know exactly what it is you want to accomplish, so you should apply this measure to all the ideas you jotted down. Talk it over with the members of your team if practicable. The result may bring to light effects you would never think of.

Applying this question to the possible suggestions usually eliminates a good many immediately. For instance, a supervisor of a maintenance crew had to work out a plan to keep his men on the job. One suggestion was to penalize them for unauthorized absence by suspending them for a day or two without pay. When he asked himself if this action would get more employees to work, the answer was obviously negative. When a man loses his temper and makes a nasty remark to his supervisor, there is an attitude problem. Someone has to decide what to do about it. The objective is to change his attitude. Would it solve the problem to bawl him out in front of the group? Sometimes this kind of test will eliminate all but one possible plan. In that case there is no alternative but to use it. In most instances, however, there is still a choice.

Feasibility. The second test is to ask, "Which action of those that accomplish the purpose is the most feasible?" To be more specific, which action is easiest to take, costs the least, can be accomplished promptly, or brings about the least confusion? You should ask such questions not only of yourself but also of other persons, particularly those who are closer to the job than you are. In planning to lacquer-finish a special order of 10,000 small parts, the foreman of a small paint shop consulted with his crew and got several suggestions on ways to do the job. After a careful analysis of the situation, he decided to rig up a dip tank because it was quick, economical, and required less change in the shop setup. He selected the most feasible action.

Sometimes ideas look good on paper, but further study may show they are not practical. They may cause worse troubles than the one they were designed to cure. They may require too much money or time, or materials may not be readily available. Or, they may be satisfactory in these respects but create troubles in other places. This point is very important. To take any action without finding out its possible effect on related operations can lead to other difficulties.

Acceptability. The final question involves other people who might be affected. Before deciding, it is always wise to ask, "How will it be accepted by others: employees, bosses, or even the public?" An action may be both suitable and feasible, but, if it creates antagonism or is resisted, it is usually doomed to failure. A decision by a board of directors to raise executive salaries seemed justified to compensate for increases in costs of living, to prevent the resignations of key people for salary reasons, and to raise morale. Furthermore, the financial position of the company made it feasible. Yet, the stockholders saw it as a move to milk the treasury and elected a new board at the first opportunity.

In an Eastern plant, the management received a few complaints about the quality of food served in the company cafeteria. The front office decided to raise all prices slightly to be able to give better and larger portions. The employees promptly boycotted the cafeteria. Here, when the effect on employees was not considered, an unacceptable decision was made, and a minor problem became a major one. These examples are not unusual. They point out how the careless executive may take action that not only fails to accomplish what he wants, but also can actually make the situation worse. To select the best answer, it pays to make sure the solution is acceptable.

To be completely honest, it must be admitted there is no way of knowing if the best solution was chosen. There may always be a better one that was not thought of. However, to the degree that your choice meets all three of the criteria, you can be assured that it will be satisfactory because it will accomplish your goal in an effective manner.

The final decision may involve some compromises, but it has to be done if you are to have a plan of action. All of the time spent in analyzing the situation, interpreting the facts, and getting ideas for possible actions is lost if you do not eventually decide upon a plan to be followed.

Modern technology is supplying some aids to the busy executive who must make many momentous decisions. With the advent of "electronic brains" a new facility of decision-making became available. Although these amazing devices cannot take the place of human intelligence, they can be of great assistance in speeding up many of the most complex and exhausting mental processes. For example, machines cannot search out the facts necessary to solve a problem or determine what information is relevant, but, once the significant data have been secured, they can be fed into the machines where interpretations and possible actions are obtained almost instantly. The training course in decision-making for top executives offered by the American Management Association uses such a device to speed up the process. This well-known "Top Management Decision Game," as a training device, actually compresses a

full decade of practice in realistically simulated business decision-making into just a few days. Big business, the only kind
of business that can afford the investment, is making increasing
use of such computers to reach the many complex determinations required in this space-probing age. But the machines
still cannot supplant the intellects of responsible managers who
must make the final decision.

THE QUALITY OF DECISION

Thus far the method by which decisions are made, or de-
cisiveness, has been emphasized. Many people have this quality
to a high degree: they can give an answer with little or no
hesitation. Unfortunately, the overly decisive person, in an
effort to impress people with this power to decide quickly, can
fall into the habit of making snap judgments. He makes many
decisions but with a high degree of error. Everyone should be
decisive in the sense that he wants to be able to give answers
when they are needed, but it is equally important to take time
to be sure they are sound answers.

This factor is the quality of decision. Every manager can
expect to make errors in judgment once in a while. It is not
pleasant to admit that one has pulled a boner, but every executive has to do it from time to time. This is part of the risk
in having the authority to make decisions. Mistakes are a matter
of averages; by planning well, the larger proportion of your
decisions should be good ones.

Knowing, then, that from time to time you may make a
mistake, what should you do about it? First and foremost, you
should acknowledge it rather than equivocate, pass the buck,
or attempt to defend yourself. And then you can take steps
to correct the situation. Nothing will enhance your reputation
as a dependable manager more than demonstrating you have

the strength of character to admit your errors and correct them. There is always reasonable leeway for allowable error; mistakes are forgivable. Furthermore, as you perceive where your thinking was at fault, you gain experience and improve your judgment for the future.

Merely to review the method by which decisions are made and to accept it is not enough. The way to become skillful in its use is to use it. Why not try it out on a few of the problems that bother you? It will be clumsy and take a long time at first, but, by practice, you can develop the skill until you can often define your problem, sort and analyze the facts, and find a solution almost automatically.

TIMING

There is also the matter of timing. If someone should ask how long it takes to make a decision, it would probably be labeled as a silly question. And yet, the time element assumes great importance. The example of executives who are so skillful they can give sound answers to many problems almost immediately was cited earlier. There are equally intelligent men who have been seeking solutions for years. Much of the research in science, politics, health, and foreign relations is a long, long process. So is research in management, materials, or methods of conducting a business. The difference, of course, is in the length of time it takes to get and interpret the pertinent facts. Sometimes they are already at hand. Other times, it may take days or even years to recognize and understand them. If you have the time to get, and the competence to analyze, all of the pertinent facts about any problem, you can always come up with a good answer. When time is limited, you have to base your decision on the facts at hand and trust that they are sufficient. To protect yourself in these cases, it is often wise to qualify your answer with such a statement as, "In the light of the facts available . . ." or "As I see it now . . ." Then everyone knows you made the best possible decision under the circumstances. If it is wrong, you need not make excuses, even though you are still accountable for the action taken.

Finally, to be useful, your answers must be timely, that is, they must come up when they are needed. A doctor does not ponder over his diagnosis until the patient dies. If a fire breaks out, no one stops to look up the regulations. Often you have to make decisions or answer questions from your team without a long time to consider. You should develop skill so your solutions are both sound and timely.

APPLYING THE DECISION

The way to make a sound decision has been reviewed up to this point. But it cannot be left there. You cannot risk wasting your efforts by failing to take the action. Yet, nearly everyone has known people who did just that. A manager who delays or otherwise fails to take the action decided upon is actually avoiding his responsibility and showing a form of weakness. A person who does not have the strength of character to carry out his decision, once it is made, should not be in a position of responsibility. These are serious conclusions. Certainly no one would want his superior to think such thoughts about him. To avoid the possibility, it is wise to look more closely at the four main reasons why such situations occur:

Procrastination

Some persons just like to put off taking action. They "never do today what can be put off until tomorrow." Delay does not bother them.

Fear of criticism

There are some who are afraid they will be criticized. They anticipate trouble and do not have the strength to take in their stride any criticism that might come. So they never take any action.

Uncertainty

Others are not sure of their answers. In other words, they have not really satisfied themselves that the answer they selected is the right one, and again they fail to act.

Vacillation

Finally, some people are faced with alternative choices so similar they cannot make up their minds about what to do. When the answers are very close, there is little to be gained by delay in applying one of the solutions, even if a coin is tossed to make the decision.

After a decision is made, the longer you delay in putting it into effect, the greater chance you take that it will never be implemented. Everyone tends to procrastinate, to avoid what may be unpleasant, or to evade responsibility, so everyone is inclined to put off making changes or initiating new actions. The successful manager recognizes these deterrents; they stimulate him to act even more promptly.

The various aspects of the control process will be considered in Chapter 9. Here it will suffice to point out once more that the best plans and most carefully made decisions do not always work out exactly as anticipated. It is good strategy, therefore, to investigate to see how the action is working out.

GROUP DECISIONS

The matter of making decisions has been discussed as though it were a purely individual action. In one sense this is true. It is a sound principle that everyone must take the full responsibility for the decisions that he makes. This applies to every person in every level of the entire organization and is a responsibility that cannot be avoided.

This does not mean you cannot, or should not, draw members of your team and fellow workers into the process. Since so much attention has been given to employer–employee relations, managers are finding they get excellent cooperation by letting employees have a part in making decisions that affect them. Many times the employees know the facts better than the managers anyway. When they feel they have honestly participated in finding the answer, they are far more ready to accept and follow it because, after all, they helped make it.

The term "consultative management" is frequently used to designate this kind of group action. It emphasizes the desirability of permitting associates to take part in planning all the way up to the final decision. Frequently, the suggestions, plans, ideas, and alternatives developed by the group lead directly to the final solution. But the decision that this *is* the action to be taken *must* come from the manager. Otherwise, as Appley [3] pointed out, the executive will find himself relegated to the position of a mere presiding officer. This theme of inviting participation in making decisions is mentioned in other chapters and is always stressed in studies of human relations in business.

[3] Lawrence A. Appley, *Management In Action*, American Management Assn., New York, 1956, p. 96.

DEVELOPING THE ABILITY

If the ability to make sound decisions when they are needed is so important, the question arises as to whether a person can develop the skill. It has been implied that it can be done. The process is not much different from many situations faced in school. There you were given problems to solve, not because the answers really made any difference, but because you were being trained to solve those problems. The teacher explained the method and set up practice situations.

Similarly, this chapter explains the method to solve problems on the job. Again, the first step is to understand the method. If it is not clear at this point, it would probably be profitable to reread the chapter. It also helps to discuss the subject with other persons, to get their help on items that are not clear, or to ensure your own understanding by explaining it to them. Until you know how decisions are arrived at, you cannot expect to develop much facility in making them.

The next step follows logically. It is the practice stage, trying it out on the day-to-day job situations. This takes will power because it is easier to use snap judgment than to accumulate pertinent facts and think through a reasonable conclusion. It will take longer, particularly at first, and will seem clumsy and awkward and not worth the effort. But, as mentioned before, nearly everyone is awkward handling a new tool. It takes practice to develop facility and smoothness. The more you use the planned method, the more skillful you will become.

This is simply an exercise in judicial thinking as a conclusion to the analytical and creative efforts made during planning. Few persons realize their capacity to think constructively. When faced with a problem, they may think it is too much trouble to make a complete analysis or fear they will make an error in judgment. It is easier to pass the buck to someone else. But each time they avoid such a responsibility they are weakening, rather than strengthening, themselves. Each time they grasp an opportunity to analyze a situation and make a decision, they are developing their managerial competence and creating a work habit of great usefulness.

There are conditions that need improvement all around, but you must recognize the circumstances that annoy you. Each one is a challenge to find a way to correct it. Many of these dissatisfactions are minor, so unimportant that they are passed over time after time. Yet each one contitutes an opportunity to practice decision-making. Even if you do make errors in judgment in these small matters, it will not be of great importance. Yet, tackling these problems will aid in learning how to solve weightier matters.

BENEFITS

To conclude, here is a brief review of the advantages that can result from developing skill in making decisions. First, the part of the operation that is your responsibility will be accomplished more efficiently. Sound decisions on operating problems speed up production and improve the quality of the work. There will be less waste and fewer errors. Backlogs will be reduced and operating costs kept to the minimum.

Your subordinates, too, will benefit directly by getting good answers to their questions when they need them. Cooperation and teamwork is encouraged when everyone knows exactly what is expected of him; occasions for complaints and grievances are reduced if the work force is guided by firm, fair decisions.

The greatest benefits will accrue to you. The constant annoyance of unsolved problems will disappear. Relations with subordinates and associates will improve. Your job responsibilities will be easier to discharge. As the quality of your judgment improves, you will be building a solid reputation as a wise manager and laying the foundation for future usefulness at a higher level. Opportunities are unlimited for men who can make wise job decisions.

SUMMARY

As in the previous chapter, the emphasis here has been on what happens within the planning phase of the management cycle. Attention was directed to the necessity of arriving at a conclusion based on relevant information and sound reasoning. The point was made that the process of making up one's mind is really fairly simple but that some decisions are very difficult, if not impossible, because all the facts are not available or put together in their proper relationships. Fortunately, this skill can be acquired by practice, so everyone has the continuing opportunity of becoming not only a decisive but also a wise person. And finally, it is important to involve others when the decisions will affect them.

4

Policies, Procedures, Programs

Although effective planning always results in a decision on the action to be taken or that none is necessary, the form of the decision may vary widely. Top management is concerned with major objectives, broad policies, sound organizational structure, financing, and effective controls. At lower levels, the emphasis is on plans for staffing, communication, procedures, coordination of work processes, and management of the work force. This does not mean there is a separation of responsibilities at any one point. Rather, it implies a gradual shift in emphasis between the top and bottom levels of management. The difference is apparent if one compares the responsibilities of the president of the company to those of a first-level foreman or gang boss.

If you will refer back to page 28 in Chapter 2, you will note there are a number of ways in which management decisions are expressed. In actual day-to-day work, there is much concern with policies and procedures and the formulation of specific programs and plans of action. Each of these are results of planning and deserve special attention.

FORMULATION OF POLICIES

Definition of policy

If a store advertises, "We will not be undersold," it is announcing an important merchandising policy to the public. It is telling what management decided as a guide to its customers in their buying. When an employer says, "Consult with your immediate supervisor before coming to me with problems that relate either to your job or to personal matters," he is establishing a policy for the guidance of his employees.

A policy then tells those to whom it is directed what they are to do if and when some particular situation arises. It provides guide lines for action. It lets everyone know exactly what action to take.

Advantages of policies

There are obvious advantages to such statements. In the first place, doubt as to the appropriate course of action is removed. No one needs to hesitate for fear of doing the wrong thing. The decision has been made, so there is no excuse for delay or failure to act. If employees know in advance what the plans are, they are more at ease and job satisfaction is increased. Operations are good because everyone knows what he is supposed to do.

Preparation of the policy statement

Policies often are in written form so the decisions will be on record and everyone concerned will understand clearly what is involved. Sometimes, they are very brief, for instance, "The facilities of the Front Street parking lot will be available to employees on May 1," is a statement of policy in one sentence. Usually, however, the subject requires more lengthy treatment. Although the format of policy statements is subject to wide variation, certain essentials are generally included.

First, because a policy is put into effect when, and if, a particular situation arises, it is necessary to define what the situation is. This is frequently covered in a general preliminary statement that makes plain under what circumstances the actions are be taken and the scope of their coverage. This section may also cite the authority under which the decision is to be carried out.

In most cases, the objectives of the policy are set forth as clearly and concisely as possible. This gives a better understanding of the purposes behind the policy and increases the chances that it will be applied intelligently. It also tells the reason why the policy is needed, thus increasing employee motivation to carry it out.

Much of the meat of such statements is often found under the heading, "Responsibilities." In this section, each person who has a part in the action is identified and given explicit directions on what to do. Of course, the policy is effective only to the extent that these duties and responsibilities are completely identified for each person.

It is not unusual to find other miscellaneous items included in a policy statement, such as references to related documents, issuances to be rescinded or superseded, or distribution data. If, however, the statement clearly sets forth the situation, the objectives to be accomplished, and the responsibilities of the persons involved, it contains the real essentials of a management policy. More informal statements may take the form of a letter to employees. Examples of both types follow:

FORMAL POLICY STATEMENT

SUBJECT: Supervisor training and development

1. General statement:

In the interest of economy and efficiency, all supervisors must be fully aware of their personnel management duties and responsibilities. To this end, provision will be made for all such employees to receive orientation, training, or retraining as necessary to achieve a high degree of competence as supervisors.

2. General policy:

It is the policy of the Company to provide the most enlightened supervision possible to its employees. It is realized by the Company that competent supervision can make the difference between satisfaction or dissatisfaction on the job and between company success or failure.

3. Objectives:

In carrying out this policy, it is desired that all concerned will strive to attain the following objectives:

a. Immediate:

To ensure a mutually satisfactory relationship between supervisors and those supervised

To permit free communication between all employees and all organizational units

To develop a feeling of pride in the Company, its practices, its products, and its contribution to the national economy

b. Long-range:

To improve relations between the work force and management officials

To increase the efficiency of operations throughout the installation

To reduce the cost of operations
To decrease turnover of employees
To enhance the contribution of each organizational segment to the total objectives of the Company

4. Responsibilities:

a. The Company will provide the following developmental services:

Furnish orientation training in the essentials of supervision to all newly appointed supervisors
Administer a more complete course in supervision following the introductory period to ensure the practice of sound supervision at all levels
Conduct management clinics on a continuing basis for all supervisors in the form of problem-solving conferences to be held not less frequently than once a month for at least one and a half hours
Provide advanced training for selected supervisors to ensure understanding of the management process and provide for the efficient use of managerial skills

b. Heads of organizational segments of the Company will:

Encourage all supervisors to take advantage of opportunities for self-development
Appraise the performance and capabilities of each supervisor reporting directly to them in order to determine directions in which improvement can be made
Discuss these findings with each supervisor and seek agreement on actions to improve supervisory practices
Consult with appropriate staff representatives to determine methods, facilities, and criteria to be used
Furnish helpful guidance and coaching to subordinate supervisors on a continuing basis
Participate as a conference leader or consultant in group training of their own or other supervisors

c. The personnel office will:

Furnish technical guidance on all such activities

Assist in necessary scheduling and procurement of training aids and other physical arrangements

Provide training to qualify executives as on– or off–the–job trainees and conference leaders

Assist in evaluation of progress of trainees and of results of the program

Conduct such parts of the group training activities as are appropriate

Maintain records, make reports, and analyze data for management as needed

INFORMAL POLICY STATEMENT

Date

To All Employees:

A discussion of the way vacation leave is handled was held at the last meeting of the Plant Committee. It was pointed out that certain inequities have developed over the years and that our plan of granting the same amount of paid vacation time to all employees who have been with the Company for more than one year is no longer satisfactory. The problem was thoroughly discussed and a recommendation made that vacation leave be granted on a sliding scale to give appropriate recognition to loyalty and length of service.

This proposal has been studied by the Board of Directors and an agreement reached on certain modifications to our present plan which, it is felt, will result in a policy that is fair to both employees and the Company.

Beginning January 1 of next year, paid vacation leave for all employees will be scheduled on the following basis:

1. Less than one year of employment   None
2. One to five years   5 days
3. Five to fifteen years   10 days
4. Fifteen to thirty years   15 days
5. More than thirty years   20 days

This change will reduce the amount of leave during the early years of employment by a modest amount but substantially extend the period for older employees. Because it follows closely the recommendations of your representatives and agrees with modern ideas of fair practice, it is hoped that the revision is in the best interests of all.

George Morris
General Manager

Policy by default

Statements of policy are frequently originated by staff men [1] who sense a need for a clearer definition of their particular programs. To secure a better understanding, they draft a document setting forth what they conceive to be the desirable policy of the organization. This may be made official by the signature of a responsible line official without any warning to those affected, and the statement reaches them through channels as merely another communication. It may be read with little or no interest or it may arouse feelings of annoyance and even resentment.

Under such circumstances, the policy has little chance of being carried out wholeheartedly. There may be no resulting impact whatsoever on management practices. In effect, the policy of the organization, as reflected in its practice, has undergone no change and remains as before the statement was issued.

---

[1] A discussion of the difference between staff and line personnel will be found in Chapter 5.

In other instances, policy statements are given wide publicity and cited by management officials as representing the existing situation. Actually, however, in the day-to-day operation of the organization, the policy may be completely ignored. The real policy is not what appears on paper but the practices carried out by the supervisors on the job. Employees are never fooled by a statement when it is at variance with the actual work situation. The latter always constitutes the *real* policy.

A third condition occurs when management people completely fail to define policy. When this happens, subordinates are forced to seek guidance from the actions of those above them. The effective or meaningful policy is set by what management officials *do*, rather than what they *say*.

There are three lessons to be learned from this. First, any policy decision should be fully explained to (and, so far as possible, agreed to by) all persons who will be affected by it. Secondly, a policy statement should never be issued unless management is prepared to see it is followed. Finally, supervisors' actions are interpreted by employees as policy decisions for their future guidance whether the supervisors intend it or not.

Involvement and coordination

In the paragraphs above it was pointed out that policies can be ignored. This results from a fundamental human characteristic: people resist changes that have no apparent value for *them*. No one likes to change his attitudes or habits. It is much easier to go along in the same old way. Unless employees can see that the proposal has some real benefit for them, they are inclined to put it aside and forget about it. All managers recognize this principle, but they do not always observe it in policy decisions.

In this regard, you have to depend upon your subordinates to see that policy is carried out. It would seem wise, then, to include those who will be affected by the decision in your planning. The more deeply they are involved, the better they will understand the advantages and the more interested they will be in having the policy carried out successfully.

During the discussions, most of the difficulties in implementing the plan will be disclosed and solutions found. What might work well in one division, may run into serious trouble in another. What would be welcomed by the day shift, may completely upset operations in the graveyard shift. Therefore, effective coordination of a policy decision throughout the entire organizational segment is essential, and full participation of subordinate officials will assist materially in achieving this goal.

Exceptions to policy

Although in theory policy tells you what to do or what someone else will do, there are occasions when it is wise to make an exception. For example, a department store had a longstanding policy of docking all employees for tardiness in excess of thirty minutes. However, one morning a hurricane so upset transportation facilities that nearly all the employees were more than an hour late and some could not get to the store at all. In this situation it was decided to make an exception and not penalize any worker who managed to get to work that day.

The question immediately arises as to whether or not the basic policy of the company was changed by this action. It would only be natural for employees to assume they would not be docked whenever a storm occurred. So an alert management takes immediate steps to notify all concerned that this was an exception and the old policy will still apply in the future. Only such positive action can maintain policy effectively after an exception has been made. Failure to make such an explanation may establish a precedent that will result in misunderstanding and impaired employee relations when the basic policy is enforced later.

PROCEDURAL STATEMENTS

Normally top management officials confine their planning to policy decisions on what to do rather than specifying procedures on how it is to be done. However, there are times, when a method is applicable to an entire organization, that a decision is made requiring its use at all lower echelons. But more frequently, the procedures that put policies into effect are worked out in the middle and lower levels.

A procedural statement, then, represents a management decision as to the way work is to be performed. Typically it is in considerable detail and specifies the methods, processes, equipment, tools, and even the movements involved. It tells where action is to take place, the sequence of operations, and the allowances permitted for error. Just as policies describe what is to be done, procedures give guidance as to how it is to be done.

Standardization

The immediate effect of an official procedural statement is to standardize the work methods to which it is applied. The decision that "this is the way to do it" establishes a pattern to be followed. Deviations from the standard procedure are frowned upon; employees are required to use the prescribed methods.

Some persons object to standard procedures because they think such requirements mean regimentation and reduction of initiative. In the best sense a procedure reflects the accepted experience to date, the know-how of previous employees, and the most satisfactory way so far discovered. Therefore, good management follows it until a more efficient method is developed.

Standard procedures are formulated for two main reasons. One is to make the most economical use of the manpower, materials, equipment, and time available. An increasing number of shops, warehouses, and offices are studying their operations to find more efficient procedures. Skilled methods engineers, both from the work force and from private consulting firms, are being called upon to streamline work processes. When a substantially more economical procedure is found, it is logical to require its use.

The other reason for standardizing work methods is for safety. Many industries deal with extremely dangerous materials and processes, all of which contain real hazards. Injuries to persons and damage to property must be avoided not only because of the cost in money and suffering but also because of the heavy production losses. There are safe and unsafe ways to work. Good management tries to find out a satisfactory, safe method and requires it to be followed. Thus, standard procedures are prescribed to save money and reduce losses due to accidents.

Effect on work force

Many times the supervisor decides how work is to be performed in his unit and, thus, establishes the procedures. Other times, standard operating procedures result from a decision made at a higher level and come down as a directive. In either case, the impact on the members of the work force must be considered.

Probably the first, and almost universal, reaction of the employee is to think "What is the sense in making this change? We have been doing all right." Although people prefer to continue in the old familiar ways, if any progress is to be made, changes are inevitable. People have to be motivated so they accept new procedures and put them into effect intelligently, willingly, and even enthusiastically.

This goes into the subject of morale—motivation, cooperation, or the will to work. Volumes have been written on it, and more will follow. Here it will suffice to suggest that when you want to introduce a change of this kind, you should make sure the employees see some sense to it. They are entitled to know why it was concocted, what advantages are anticipated, and how it will affect them.

If you originate the new method yourself, you certainly have brought all of your key subordinates in on the planning. If the procedure comes from above, you should still involve this same group in the plans you must make to put it into effect.

An important effect of standard procedures is to restrict the initiative of employees. Americans are noted for their strong individualism; they like to be able to do things in their own way. The older, highly skilled workmen particularly may resent being told how to perform their work. No one wants to become a robot if he can help it.

In most businesses it is a firmly established policy that working conditions should provide employees with the greatest possible job satisfaction. Yet, as work methods are standardized, much of the basis for such satisfaction is taken away. The workers no longer have the opportunity to decide for themselves how the task is to be performed. Every procedure that requires a standard method to be followed limits the initiative of the workers involved.

This is, of course, simply another example of the effect of

standards on freedom. In this case, freedom to choose the way in which one is going to do his job. The "efficiency-minded" executive is inclined to overlook the effects of standardization on the individuals who make up the work force; he is not at all concerned about the results of over-regimentation of employees. However, most management officials today are just as concerned with the morale of their work force as with their work processes. They use good judgment in introducing standard procedures so employees will not feel that they are being reduced to mere cogs in the machine. In fact, recent studies reveal that specialization and standardization, if carried too far, result in lower rather than higher productivity.

Introducing new procedures

The necessity of conditioning employees to changes in work methods has already been pointed out: they are the ones who eventually put the new procedure into operation and its success or failure to a large degree is literally in their hands.

Getting an individual or a group ready to make a change in work processes involves more than just announcing the change. Even careful explanations of the reasons "why" are not enough. Although maintaining morale and job satisfaction are important factors, you must also make sure that every single employee is able to carry out his part efficiently.

Almost invariably, the introduction of new procedures requires a thorough review of the competence of the workers involved in relation to the requirements of the new method. Different tasks have to be performed in a different manner. At this point, the supervisor is faced with a basic question, "Do the members of the work force possess the necessary knowledge and skill to operate the new procedure efficiently?"

The answer is seldom an unequivocal yes. More often, when

you compare the qualifications of your employees to the requirements of the new plan, you find a clearly defined need for some job training. Probably the whole group should be brought together for an explanation of the change and an opportunity to get answers to any aspects that are not clear. Possibly a well-planned conference on "How are we going to make this change?" would be desirable. No doubt some individuals will need special training in their parts of the operation. You may be able to send some to observe, or even work for a time in, a section where the new procedure has been installed, or you may have to spend time in individual coaching on the job. You may want to send certain people to formal training courses. If the new method is going to succeed, you have to make certain that each employee is able to handle his part of the process satisfactorily.

PROGRAM PLANNING [2]

The outcome of planning as represented by management decisions on both policies and procedures has been discussed in some detail. Policies and procedure were treated separately to keep clear the basic differences between them. In actual practice, however, "what to do" can seldom be separated from "how to do it." There are procedural implications in all policy statements. Procedures have to involve the policy they are designed to implement.

Much of the planning in business centers around programs or plans of action in which both policy and procedure are spelled out for the guidance of everyone concerned. They

[2] A program is generally considered to be a stable plan of action that continues over an extensive period of time. A project, on the other hand, is more limited, involving a single, specific plan of action that reaches a conclusion and is completed. However, what is said on program planning is equally applicable to project planning.

usually originate fairly high in the organization and contain both policy and procedure because lower echelons require such guidance to know what to do and how to do it. Some program planning, however, goes on at every level in an organization, whether it is called a "program" or simply a plan of action. At lower levels, the scope is necessarily narrower but the intent to get something accomplished in a specific way is the same, such as a recreation program or a building maintenance program.

Understanding purpose and policy

Again, before a plan for action can be made, the planners must have the specific objectives and the policy to be followed clearly in mind. Management must decide the purpose of the action and what actions are required to reach that goal.

Unfortunately, people sometimes start planning without a clear understanding either of their objective or of the policy to be followed. Such planning may start merely from an executive's expression of dissatisfaction with some condition. Without mature judgment and managerial competence, his staff may initiate action that will accentuate rather than relieve the situation. Because plans of action affect many people, all programs must be firmly based on clear objectives and sound policies.

Determining requirements and capabilities

After these basic factors are defined, it is possible to view the proposed program from the point of view of getting it accomplished or the procedural aspect. Most operations involve fundamental problem of supply. Knowing now what the plan is, the question arises as to what will be the requirements to carry it out.

Requirements take many forms: material, manpower, electricity, transportation, or scientific know-how. Estimates, based on experience, have to be made of how much of each item is necessary for the operation of the program. Some may be on hand, others in warehouses. Certain items may have to be procured.

The need to purchase materials or equipment raises other problems. "Are they available on the market? Will this particular type have to be manufactured? Could any substitutes be used? Are funds available to purchase them?" Questions of this kind must be answered affirmatively before the program is feasible.

If large quantities are needed, the ability of industry to supply the need must be considered; the national productive capacity has definite limits. For instance, with existing facilities only so much oil can be produced in a year. Much of it is required by the government. The persons who plan the defense programs for the nation must make sure their requirements do not create a drastic scarcity that could inflate costs and cause serious economic conditions.

Deterrents and obstacles

Hints and definite indications of troubles to be encountered will emerge in the development of any program. Both need to be explored. Some of these difficulties, such as procurement problems and resistance to change, have been noted before. These obstacles should be identified as much as possible so they can be avoided or overcome.

In the planning process, analysis of the situation usually discloses many of the conditions that would deter effective action. Program-planning conferences bring together the experiences of others in similar situations and help identify obstacles. Most of the really serious hindrances should be identified and dealt with in planning, or the program runs a great risk of failure.

Control factors

One of the procedural aspects that must be included in program planning is how to ensure the objectives being achieved after the plan goes into action. Usually some reporting or inspection techniques must be used as a check on progress. Often detailed standards and criteria are set forth in the program document. Frequently it is desirable to break the plan of action into phases with time requirements for each part. Management officials are able to keep a check on the program operation with such devices and take quick action to correct any situation that appears to endanger its success.

A basic control on all program planning is inherent in budget limitations. Fiscal controls are particularly significant in view of the necessity for annual reporting to stockholders and to the Internal Revenue Service. All modern business depends on a carefully planned budget and on accurate accounting systems that ensure operation within the budget limitations.

SUMMARY

Modern business could not exist on a haphazard basis. Each aspect of operations is planned well in advance. The goals are carefully defined; much time is spent formulating clear statements of what will be done and, to varying degrees, how it will be done. These program and project statements plot the course of the organization. They provide specific guides to employees at all levels in the organization so operations will be performed efficiently and safely. The more competently the planning is done, the greater the assurance that the goals will be achieved efficiently and economically.

PART THREE

Taking Executive Action

After the decisions have been made as a result of careful planning, action must follow or the purposes of the business enterprise will not be achieved. Three important processes necessary to get action under way are described in this section. They are: the organization of the resources, the directions to the workers, and the coordination of all efforts into a smooth operation.

5

The Nature of Organization

The preceding four chapters covered one of the major segments of the management cycle: the planning and decision-making stage. The next major phase is taking executive action. The guiding theory in this study is that good management requires thinking through what one is going to do in conducting any kind of an enterprise before setting the wheels in motion. The course of action is decided on the basis of this planning.

Whether you are concerned with a single work order, the installation of a new office procedure, or the activation of a new plant, you are faced with certain organizational problems at a very early stage. In fact, as soon as you have decided what you have to do, you should begin to organize the facilities and resources to carry out the plan efficiently. As has been pointed out several times before, this requires additional planning and decisions on how the best organization can be set up. Planning and replanning continue throughout the entire management cycle.

THE MEANING OF THE ORGANIZING PROCESS

Organization has been necessary since men began working together to accomplish common purposes. It results from the search for a more effective way to get something done. As long as one individual does a job by himself there is little need for organizing, but, when several persons enter the activity cooperatively, someone must take charge and become responsible. At the risk of oversimplification, it might be said that the process of organization is the determination of internal relationships to clarify lines of authority, flow of work, and channelling of information. The aspects of the process that help understanding of the nature of what goes on in organizing or reorganizing work operations are considered here from this point of view.

The objectives of an organization

Although objectives as goals or purposes of an enterprise were discussed in Chapter 2, they will be explored more fully here. Until and unless there is a clearly defined purpose for an enterprise, there is, of course, no reason for organization. In other words, men organize to accomplish a specific objective. Setting the goal must come first. The clearer the goal in the minds of the organizers and the better it is interpreted in terms of their common understanding, the better the various relationships will be defined. In many situations, in fact in nearly every situation, a clearer understanding of the reasons for the organization is obtained by putting the objectives in writing. The Preamble to the Constitution clearly states the purpose of the organization to be effected by that instrument. Corporation charters are always required to state specifically and in detail the objectives of the corporate structure.

The objectives influence organization at every level. The major goal of any enterprise is general in nature and looks toward the final outcome of the combined activities necessary to accomplish it. This is supplemented by a series of secondary objectives for each subordinate unit. Thus, from top to bottom, each operating unit has its own special purpose and its own organization to get the job done.

Finally, it should be remembered that objectives are not necessarily fixed, inflexible goals. Revised or even new goals are frequently needed as conditions change. Changes in methods, materials, work products, or locations force changes in an organization. New conditions may also set up aims, or a new board chairman may insist upon new interpretations of the program. Sometimes the pressure of public opinion can effect marked shifts in purpose. Whenever the purpose changes, the organizational structure must be brought into line with the new objective or the goal probably will never be reached. This means an organization must be flexible enough to be modified to carry out revised objectives.

THE EFFECT OF WORK SPECIALIZATION

As the relationships betwen the units of an organization are determined, the total pattern begins to take form. In a real sense, the organizer is building a structure because he first identifies and separates the constituent parts and then ties them firmly together again in their proper relationships.

An illustration of how this worked out in a simple job situation that became complex is the shoe industry. Not too many years ago, all shoes were made by hand. John was a shoemaker and a good one. When he got more business than he could take care of alone, he hired several apprentices to assist him and to learn the trade. As soon as each one became proficient, he was given a bench and, like his employer, made shoes, from heel to toe and from sole to upper. The picture looked like this:

As time went on, John began to notice a marked difference in the quality of work turned out by the boys. Tom was particularly good at working on soles. Dick, on the other hand, was excellent in handling upper work; and Harry did an outstanding job of assembling and finishing shoes. Instead of nagging his workers about the tasks they did *not* do as well as the others, John decided to have each one do the particular thing he did best. He assigned Tom to prepare the soles, Dick to work on the uppers, and Harry to assemble and finish them.

Much to John's gratification, under the new specialization plan not only were the shoes superior in quality, but there was also a surprising increase in production. John was forced to give up his place at the bench and devote his time to securing leather, making deliveries, parcelling out the work, inspecting it, collecting his payments, and handling other nonproduction activities. Despite this, he found he was making a greater profit.

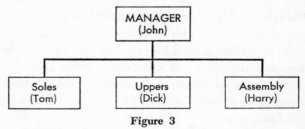

Figure 3

He had specialized the jobs, set up an organization, and, in a small way, had become a manager.

The organization could be pictured as in Figure 3 as a result of delegating the work *just one step*.

This does not finish the story, however. Because of the superior workmanship and fast service resulting from the new organization, business increased. Soon John had to hire several additional workers to assist the three original employees. These new men required considerable attention, and John was unable to carry the burden alone. It was not long before Tom, Dick, and Harry spent most of their time supervising the new workers in their departments. The situation became a little more complicated as indicated in Figure 4.

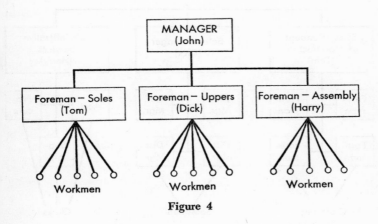

Figure 4

This idea of greater specialization, further delegation, and increasingly complex organization can be carried on almost indefinitely. Eventually some employees might be working exclusively on men's shoes and others on women's or children's. Special units could be set up to handle calf leather, kid, dress, or work shoes. Eventually John would need help in keeping books, purchasing, warehousing, advertising, selling, and possibly legal matters. Each such step means more complex work relationships and a more intricate organizational structure.

In Figure 4, John appointed three supervisors to whom he made an actual delegation of some of his authority, so he now directly supervises only three employees. Each of these three directly supervises other employees with whom John has only an indirect relationship. As the organization grows larger, more supervisors are appointed and more of John's authority

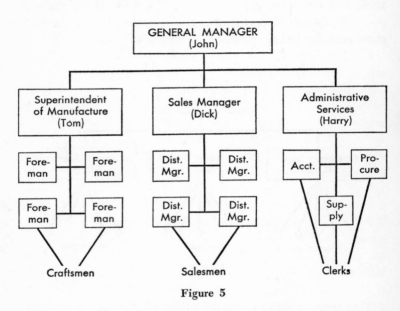

Figure 5

is delegated. This process can continue until John finds he cannot give proper attention to the problems raised by the supervisors under his direct control. At this time, he will need to establish an addiitonal level of supervision, thus reducing the number of employees receiving direct supervision from him so he can again exercise adequate leadership and supervision. The new organization might look like Figure 5.

Delegation of responsibility and authority

The same illustration can be duplicated in many occupations. As John developed from a skilled craftsman to a successful administrator, he encountered all the problems managers have to solve. The organizational aspect was emphasized to show how John was forced to call on his subordinates to share his heavy management responsibilities as the business grew.

A similar situation occurs in every growing enterprise. Executives find there are not enough hours in the day to do the planning and make the decisions that are necessary. Much has been written, and far more said, about the terrific burden of executive responsibility. Ulcers, heart attacks, nervous breakdowns, and early deaths have come to typify the "successful" executive. It is a sad state of affairs indeed when a person has to sacrifice his health or even his life to maintain his livelihood.

Fortunately, people are beginning to realize such situations need not exist; in fact, they usually indicate poor management. These conditions develop because the executive has not organized his own job efficiently and has not delegated part of his responsibilities to others to relieve himself of the excess burden.

There are a number of reasons why this happens. Probably the main one is that many persons like to make all of the decisions themselves. It contributes to their feeling of importance. They find it difficult to give up a task they are accustomed to performing. Or they think their subordinates are not as competent and, hence, would not do the work as well. They have never found time to develop the necessary abilities in their employees, so they cannot delegate responsibilities to them. Such men do not see they never will become really successful executives simply because they are not managing their own activities efficiently. They are caught in a vicious circle, and they will have even less time to manage their operations.

It all comes back to a question of how the executive can utilize his time, energy, and ability to best advantage. A simple analysis of what a man is doing, made over a brief period of time, usually discloses certain tasks that a subordinate could do equally well. True, the subordinate may need some training, but once he learns how to do the work, the boss has lightened his own burden to that extent. In the future he will only have to check occasionally to be sure the task is being performed properly.

When a management official finds his job is beginning to wear him down, he has a clear signal to take stock of his work pattern. He must reduce the demands upon him to a point where he can manage efficiently. Not only his personal success is at stake but also the success of the operation for which he is responsible. Delegation of the more routine aspects of his work is often the answer.

What can he delegate? The answer lies in the situation itself. A careful analysis of the job as it exists will disclose the particular duties or tasks that can be assigned to subordinate employees. There are, however, a few common-sense criteria that can be applied.

The tasks should be such that, with reasonable training, the employee can perform them satisfactorily.

They should be time-consuming activities that will appreciably relieve the burden of the executive.

Ordinarily they are duties of a more routine, rather than policy-making, nature.

They should not cause the subordinate to be overburdened.

Finally, if an employee is asked to be responsible for a duty his boss has been performing, he should have the authority necessary to discharge that responsibility. This point is frequently overlooked. Executives forget that their subordinates normally do not have the same authority they do. The employee may not only be embarrassed, but also his efforts may be completely frustrated because he cannot get what is needed to carry out the assignment. This is why, in any major delegation of work as in other types of assignment, it is desirable to put the matter in writing and include the specific authority needed to accomplish the work.

Decentralization

Another closely related aspect of organization is decentralization of major segments of the work to lower echelons with full responsibility for performance. This situation is not concerned with a personal duty of one individual being delegated to a specific subordinate employee. Instead, the transfer of whole processes or broad responsibilities from one organizational level to a lower one is considered. For instance, the main office of a firm decides that the review and processing of certain contracts should be performed in the field instead of at headquarters, or responsibility for fund control is placed in each operating division instead of being handled in the office of the controller.

The bigger an enterprise gets, the more necessary it is to shift responsibilities and operations downward. The organization has to change with each such change because one level loses a function and another picks it up. But, this is not all; the higher echelon has to set up some control to be sure the operation is properly carried out.

American industry today is typically big business. As such, it has extremely difficult problems of organization. Changes are constantly going on to improve the relationships between the segments, to keep channels of communication open, and to get the work accomplished efficiently. As businesses continue to grow, the tendency for more decentralization increases.

THE HUMAN ELEMENT IN ORGANIZATION

In theory, organization deals with the work to be done rather than with the people who do it. A department is formed because certain closely related tasks fit together logically to make a major contribution in the accomplishment of the work. The organizational pattern is based on the grouping together of the functions, duties, tasks, and processes that go together most naturally.

It is not always easy to determine where a specific activity belongs. "Would it be better to have all minor motor repairs made by the unit to which the vehicle is assigned or to have a separate automotive maintenance shop for all cars? Should inspections be made by employees in each of the operating units or by a special group of inspectors? Should advertising be part of sales or a separate department?"

Questions of this kind cannot always be answered without referring to the people concerned. Although theory says to establish the organization and then staff it with competent people, the situation seldom works out quite so simply. In most instances at least some of the personnel are already at hand and have to be considered. Human beings cannot be handled like blocks of wood, discarding those that do not fit the plan. The people who are available to fill the jobs established in the organizational structure have to be considered.

In setting up a new unit or in reorganizing an established one, the first concern is filling the key jobs. To do this, it is necessary to know: First, the actual job knowledge, skills, and attitudes required of the employee to carry on the operation satisfactorily; and secondly, the real abilities, competence, and pertinent characteristics of the people available.

The objective, of course, is to select a person who has the necessary leadership to make the operation a success. However, it is seldom possible to get a perfect fit. There are almost always substantial differences between the capacity of the employee under consideration and the requirements of the job. Frequently the choice narrows down to one individual who does not quite meet all of the specifications.

In such a situation, there are three main ways by which the organizer can reduce the differences between the individual's capacity and the demands of the position. The first is to give carefully planned training in the specific job aspects where the person needs assistance. This helps fit the man to the job. Secondly, the organizer can take another look at the job itself to see if it can be changed to meet the qualifications of the man without upsetting the organizational plans.

Finally, it is sometimes possible to give the employee special assistance in the aspects of the work where he lacks experience. This method is usually needed only temporarily because the worker should gain experience and competence rapidly under careful supervision on the job. Assigning an acting assistant who is strong in the areas where the new man needs help is often effective.[1] Sometimes the executive in charge can hold back the assignment of some of the responsibilities until the appointee develops the necessary competence in these directions. This puts an additional burden on the executive, but normally it is only for a brief period and gives him the incentive to make sure conditions are most favorable to develop the subordinate into a fully qualified leader.

[1] Careful supervision in this situation is extremely important, or the developing executive may come to lean on the assistant as on a crutch.

GUIDES FOR ORGANIZING

In the last chapter some of the problem areas to be considered in planning an organizational structure were reviewed. These matters have been studied seriously over the years to find a pattern that would help management officials do an effective job in planning. Although a poor organization often gets along fairly well if the people in it make it work, it is equally true that a better-planned structure accomplishes far better results. Some guides for better organizing results follow.

Basis for organization

There are several different ways in which executives can approach their organizational planning. The four main directions are to set up a structure:

1. On the basis of the broad functions to be performed
2. On the basis of the specific operations required
3. On the basis of the place where the work is to be done and
4. On the basis of the various products handled or services rendered.

It is quite common to find purchasing, manufacturing, and sales as the primary operating departments in business. They represent the basic functions of procurement, fabrication, and disposal of the product. Service organizations, such as banks and insurance companies, however, do not have a manufacturing function. An organization is often patterned on the basis of the functions to be performed. As American business grows larger and competition becomes more keen, it is more and more common to find research units, engineering departments, and production planners.

Setting up a structure based on operations is a little different.

This method is mainly used to bring together all the operations of the same kind. For instance, it might be more efficient to have all stenographers together in a central clerical pool to be used when needed by any of a group of executives rather than assign a secretary to each one. In a similar way, transportation operations may be organized by establishing a motor pool. Instead of each department or branch having its own attorney, a central legal office may be set up to serve all departments. A maintenance division eleminates the necessity of keeping carpenters, plumbers, electricians, and painters at each point where their services might be needed. Organizing on the basis of the operation to be performed is a sound practice because it brings together closely related jobs and usually permits more economical utilization of the work force.

As businesses and industries grow, geography often has a significant part in determining where parts of the organization are located. Accessibility of sources of supply can be as important as available markets. Climate can also play a big part in the success of the enterprise, as can power, water supply or transportation. Entire industries have been moved to secure cheaper labor. Even in small businesses, some operations may have to be segregated because of noise, fumes, or danger to personnel.

Finally, it is standard practice to have separate plants to produce different items. General Motors Corp. produces each make of its cars separately. Westinghouse Electric Corp. builds refrigerators in one part of the organization and television sets in another. Department stores are organized to a major degree on the basis of the products sold.

The student of organization as a management process will readily recognize that these four factors must be considered in setting up a sound structure. It should be equally apparent that managers frequently use all four in determining the best setup for a particular purpose. All of these factors may even be used within a single department to establish an efficient organizational pattern.

Types of organizational components

Because the reason for organization is to clarify the relationships between the various units of an enterprise, it is necessary to determine what the major units of accomplishment are and then to analyze each of them in turn. This process is not entirely thought through from the top down, however. It is also necessary to consider the relationships from the bottom up. Otherwise, the resulting structure may be theoretically correct but impractical in operation. As the structure takes form, is modified, corrected, or changed in the light of additional facts about work relationships, it always begins to reflect lines of authority. This is because the organization indicates who reports to whom.

At this stage in the plan of organization, the line relations are being developed. Line functions are those through which authority is exercised to accomplish the objective of the enterprise. Each has its own special part in getting the job of the company done properly and on time. Thus, line organizations are often referred to as operating units and the people in charge of these activities as operating officials. This distinguishes such functions from staff or auxiliary functions.

Probably the best differentiation between line and staff units is in the military forces where there is a clear distinction between line officers with troops and the staff units. The distinction is not always as clear in a civilian organization. However, it is only necessary to realize that there are various kinds of work to be performed in any large organization and that these differences in kind of assignment exist.

As an enterprise grows, the responsibilities of management also grow. One well-known analyst suggested that administrators may have as many as seven basic functions, which he summarized in the term P-O-S-D-CO-R-B. When a man is responsible for the Planning, Organizing, Staffing, Directing, COordinating, Reporting, and Budgeting [2] of a concern, it is no wonder that he may find himself sadly overworked. In such situations, it is common to call in specialized assistance acting in an advisory capacity to the administrative head. Frequently there is a need for a health expert, and a medical unit is set up. The employment function may be delegated to a personnel officer. Legal or financial advisers may be needed. In many businesses today, top executives have management service units as integral parts of their offices.

These extensions of the administrator-manager function, usually referred to as staff units, are under the direct supervision of the executive himself. They are responsible for securing basic data and making recommendations to him on action to be taken. In this capacity, staff units are not part of the work operations of the enterprise; they actually function as part of the administrative head. They do not give orders to operating personnel unless they speak for the executive and with his authority. In most cases they work out the plans and submit them to the boss who signs and issues them under his authority. In the long run, he assumes the responsibility for the quality of these decisions because he is the administrator.

As expansion continues, the advisability of concentrating certain duties into individual units to increase efficiency of operation is often recognized.

This may result in either line or staff units or in functions

[2] The two new functions here are "staffing," which may be included under planning and organizing, and "budgeting," which is related to planning and control.

that are a combination of both. An example is the maintenance function. This work is not directly connected with the primary mission of the organization nor is it wholly an advisory job. It assists the operating divisions in carrying out their functions more easily and takes some of the administrative and maintenance burden away from management. On the other hand, it does carry on certain operations that are closely connected with the line units and advises management in its own field. Such units are usually designated as auxiliary or service departments.

In the paragraphs above it is implied that the line part of the organization exercises the authority, giving orders to subordinate levels. This would indicate that a staff unit does not give directions to other parts of the organization. Yet in actual practice, staff offices exercise a considerable amount of authority. The medical officer sends an employee home because the man is not fit for work. The personnel manager refuses to discharge an employee summarily because the union contract requires a thirty-day notice. These are staff officers making management decisions that affect the line. On the surface, the theory of authority residing in the line seems to break down. However, a more thorough examination of the situation does not bear this out.

As previously stated, staff offices are set up to relieve the top executive of certain operating tasks. Thus, in effect, they become additional hands and brains for the administrative head. They save his time by making studies and giving the recommendations necessary to keep that part of his responsibilities going smoothly. Normally these recommendations are that some action must be followed. When the boss decides to accept the recommendation, it is common for him to designate the staff unit in question to carry out the action for him. In other words, he delegates the authority of his line position to the staff unit. When staff officers use authority in this manner, it is always based on a specific act of delegation: they are using the authority of the administrator rather than that which is inherent in their function.

One other aspect of these relationships, the so-called "functional supervision" exercised by staff officers deserves attention. It is common to find the same activities at different levels in the organization. Such functions as controller, personnel, and safety are examples. These staff units exist in the main office, regional headquarters, and individual plants. At each level, the office in question is under the management authority of the line official who directs the operation. This official is responsible for the quality of personnel and programs in these staff areas. But, in each such instance, the higher level office has a functional responsibility to provide technical leadership, guidance, and assistance to the lower echelon. This type of functional supervision does not imply that representatives of the higher staff echelon will give orders to the subordinate unit. They are restricted to providing appropriate help and advice. When their recommendations are ignored or improperly applied, the remedy is to report the circumstances to their line superior who then takes appropriate action through line channels. In this way the staff relationship is observed and technical know-how utilized to good advantage.

PRINCIPLES OF ORGANIZATION

As any enterprise becomes larger and more complex, management must plan more carefully for a smooth organization so efforts are properly directed to accomplish the objectives and the entire operation is coordinated and controlled. As part of management, every supervisor and executive shares a part of this responsibility. For effective results, each one must organize the operations for which he is responsible. Certain principles are generally used as guides in organization. Again, it should be kept in mind that even a poor organization can get results if the people concerned want it to, but there is always a better way by which competent management can secure superior results.

The following statements are generally accepted truths, but, like all generalizations, each may have exceptions. This does not, however, make them less useful as guides to sound organization. In this connection, note particularly the last item.

Some principles of organization

1. Each organization should be formed to accomplish a definite purpose.

2. So far as possible, an enterprise should be organized around the operations necessary to achieve the purpose rather than around the people available for the jobs.

3. There should be a clear line of formal authority running from the top to the bottom of every organization.

4. In every case, sufficient authority should be delegated to a subordinate to enable him to discharge his responsibilities.

5. No employee, occupying a single position in the organization, should be subject to orders from more than one source.

6. Higher authority should be responsible for the acts of its subordinates.

7. A supervisor should never have more subordinates reporting to him than he can direct effectively in view of the complexity of the work situations and the abilities and personal characteristics of the supervisor and the supervised.

8. A final goal of all organization should be to achieve smooth and effective coordination.

9. Any principle of organization should be subject to modi-

fication in terms of feasibility and the necessities of the situation.

In the light of the previous discussion, most of these statements are probably acceptable. Number seven, however, deserves a further explanation. This is often referred to as the principle of the span of control. It applies two ways. In one direction it means a supervisor or executive should have enough subordinates and activities under his direction to keep him fully occupied at his proper level of management. In the other, it means an official should not be loaded with so many subordinates that some will not get the leadership they need. Obviously, no rule can be made as to the exact number of individuals who should report to one person. Rather, the span will vary in accordance with such factors as:

the experience and ability of the supervisor
the abilities (skills and knowledge) of those supervised
the complexity of the work
the temperament and personal characteristics of the supervisor and the supervised
the physical distance between individuals being supervised.

Many persons have tried to formulate principles of organization, and many statements are available. More meaningful statements may come as a result of further study and better understanding of the process. This is only to say that the processes of management are still subject to investigation, analysis, and interpretation.

SUMMARY

An important outcome of the planning process is the organizational structure of the enterprise. Forming the organization requires a clear understanding of the primary and secondary goals, an intelligent analysis of the operations to be performed bringing together the parts that are most naturally related and delegating to competent persons the responsibility and authority to operate these segments efficiently. A number of so-called principles of organization are widely accepted as guides, but there is still controversy between students of management about their feasibility. It is reasonable to expect continued research in this field and a clearer understanding of the process as the results of these studies in real situations are applied.

6

Organizing for Effective Action

Organizing for effective action is the process of securing an orderly arrangement of equipment, procedures, and work force in their proper relationships for the efficient accomplishment of an agreed purpose. The key words are orderly arrangement, relationship, and purpose. The general nature of the organization process was discussed in the preceding chapter. Some of the more detailed aspects will be described here.

DEFINING THE ORGANIZATION

After the structure is decided by organizational planning, it is necessary to make this decision known. Probably the most common method of portraying relationships is with charts. One type of industrial organization might be represented by a chart similar to Figure 6.

Such a chart resembles somewhat the roots of a tree. The trunk divides itself into a few main roots, and these in turn are divided into smaller roots, until finally there are the root clusters that are the real support of the tree. They not only hold it securely to the ground, they also gather the water and substance from the soil to nourish the entire tree. Although the larger roots have an important function to perform and are indispensable, the small root clusters do the real work. The same is true in organization. The real production or services come from the basic units, so it is important to know

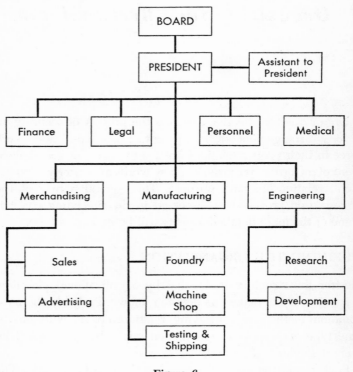

Figure 6

the support that is expected from each unit (the work *your* units do) and how it is related to the work of other units to support the main operation. Such charts are widely used because the organizational plan becomes clearer and more useful when put on paper so it can be seen and studied in relation to the objectives and problems.

More specifically, the values can be stated as:

1. Showing:
    How the authority of the administrative head is divided by related functions and assigned to a number of people
    How authority is divided and assigned according to responsibility
    What the lines of authority are
    Who assigns the work to each unit and to whom a supervisor reports or asks for help and assistance
2. Assisting to:
    Keep lines of authority straight
    Prevent confusion in giving or receiving instructions
    Show relationships between units.

In addition to the use of charts, management officials usually spell out the pattern of the organizational structure in words. Many companies have organization manuals in which the duties and responsibilities of each individual segment are carefully defined. Used in conjunction with charts, these statements tell the part played by each unit in accomplishing the total purpose.

THE SUPERVISOR'S RESPONSIBILITY
FOR ORGANIZING

It is scarcely necessary to discuss the importance and values of a well-organized operation. Much of the organizing for a large establishment is done outside of the work unit; that is, many decisions, policies, and procedures are formulated at higher levels. However, each executive or supervisor still has a great deal of responsibility in organizing his own work and the work of his unit. The following is an outline of some of the organization work that may be left to a supervisor.

Dividing work and placing responsibility among groups supervised

In organizing the work of a unit, a supervisor must decide how the work will be divided between groups and subgroups for the purpose of administration, assignment of work, direction of activities, and coordination and control of operations. He must then decide how best to arrange the groups and subgroups in relation to each other so the plans can be carried out in the most effective manner. Unit organization charts may be drawn so these relationships are known and understood by all concerned.

Assigning and arranging space and equipment

Besides the division, regrouping, and assignment of work, there are material things such as equipment and work space that must also be divided, assigned, and arranged. This can also be charted so the organization of material and flow of work is better understood. Material items to which attention must be given are:

1. Quarters available and suited to the work of the unit
   a. Construction of building or space to be occupied, such as:
      Light and heat for clerical or office use
      Strong foundation and floors for shop work
   b. Size:
      Large enough to accommodate equipment and workers and permit good arrangement of equipment

Small enough to conserve space and reduce movements

2. Equipment or machines
   a. Selected and assigned for:
      Specific steps in the work of unit
      Variety of related processes
      General work of unit
   b. Arranged to provide: [1]
      Safe operation
      Space to work
      Flow from one process to the next
      Least possible movement of material in process
      Smooth operation within unit

Assigning workers to jobs

The efforts of a number of people are usually needed to accomplish the work of a unit. They are assigned to the work they can do best. Some assignments may require several people, while others may use only one or two workers to advantage at one time. The supervisor must organize the work and assign workers so all are fully occupied and so all of the processes are carried on in proper sequence.

Several people with different skills or abilities may be working together, depending upon the kind of assignment. For example, in the salvage department of a heavy construction firm several laborers may be used to wreck heavy equipment. They mainly need the physical strength to use wrenches and wrecking bars. A few employees may be assigned to cart or carry parts to storage bins or junk piles. A crane operator may

[1] The arrangement and organization of equipment to fit into assigned space, when planned on paper, is known as a layout chart. This technique will be discussed in Chapter 11, Improving Work Methods.

be needed to move heavy parts, and some clerks may be required to keep records and prepare inventories. In an operation of this kind, workers may be assigned to dismantle or wreck a number of different types of machines or pieces of equipment at the same time. The supervisor must decide how many men are needed to dismantle a bulldozer or power shovel, how many of them should be laborers, and what other abilities are needed. On the other hand, it is obvious that in taking jeep engines apart, the number of workers and kinds of abilities needed are not the same as for heavy equipment.

The supervisor must decide how many men are needed in each assignment or job. Knowing how many workers he has and what is to be done, he must decide how many jobs to start at one time. In a large unit, it is advantageous for the supervisor to prepare a rough organization chart as he works on his plans to show how he expects to organize and assign his work force.

The purpose of the chart is to be sure skills are properly used, that enough workers with the right abilities are assigned to each job, that all necessary parts or steps of the operation are in process, and that unnecessary, or surplus, workers are not assigned to any job. The proper type of organization will result in better production records and a feeling of confidence in the supervisor.

REORGANIZING A UNIT

Opportunities to start from scratch and plan a completely new operation are limited. Most executives and supervisors run into organizational problems in the reorganization of an existing activity. The general principles still apply, but there are some aspects of changing an operation that deserve special attention. First, however, here is a review of some of the points made earlier to form a background.

A reorganization, like other kinds of change, often comes about because you recognize that operations are not set up as well as they might be. Your dissatisfaction grows until you decide to do something. In this instance, the initiative for the change comes from yourself although it may have been stimulated by someone else.

On the other hand, organizational change also comes about because of a management decision at a higher level. Such determinations may affect objectives, policies, procedures, manpower, or funds available. They may arise out of conclusions reached by executives from study of current available data or from special organization or management surveys. In any case, they may require changes in your setup.

In reorganization, too, you should keep in mind what was said about natural human resistance to change. If it is your own idea that is to be put into operation, you have the opportunity to include in the planning all those who will be affected. If the change is directed from above, you can get the same group to help plan how to make the change. The best way to get people to accept a reorganization plan is to involve them in it so they understand it and want to make it work well.

Finally you should remember what was said about the human factor in organization. For the most part, reorganization will make use of the personnel already on the job. There may be reassignments, additional training, even a few new employees, but the actual work force will remain pretty much the same. Therefore, any contemplated changes will have to take the abilities and capacities of these people into consideration. Considerable compromise may be needed between the desired structure and the one that will work best with the people available.

Now the question arises of what you actually do in reorganizing a unit and how you go about it. The following points are arranged in the order in which you would most likely approach the problem.

Estimating the situation

Whether the decision for the change is your own or that of someone else, you must start with a clear understanding of what you are trying to do, that is, the objective or purpose of the change. Certainly you do not shift your organization just for the fun of it, and unless there is a sound reason, you dare not risk upsetting an operation. But, unless the purpose is clear, you cannot plan any effective action to achieve it, and you should not be satisfied with such broad generalizations as "better employee utilization" or "increased production." You should express your purpose in terms of the specific improvements that you expect to secure: to eliminate one typist position in X section, to speed up sorting of incoming mail, to reduce material haul from machine shop to assembly, to secure better technical direction of research activities, or to reduce the management burden of the shipping department foreman.

The establishment of a definite goal enables you to see more clearly the operations, processes, and tasks needed to attain it. Here you should use your own experience and that of others. No organization can be perfected in a vacuum. The technical understanding of what is necessary to accomplish the purpose must be there. The better you understand your job, the easier it is to figure out the kinds of work that have to be performed and the job skills and knowledge required. You will also begin to see the level of abilities needed and the needs for space, equipment, services, and supplies. At this point you are making a preliminary or tentative estimate of the requirements.

Before you proceed much further, it is usually wise to make a critical review of operations under the present organization. This may show that you can accomplish your purpose with only minor modification. Assuming, however, a major change is necessary, an assessment of the current job situation will reveal the nature, direction, and extent of change that are needed. Such a study clearly reviews both the human and material resources that are available, providing you with a better idea of what you have to work with. It may also disclose hindrances or obstacles to be overcome before any reorganization can be successful.

Grouping the new jobs

So far, you have made a rather thorough analysis of the problem, and determined what you want to accomplish, the direction in which changes must be made, and what you have to work with. Now you can start a synthesis—putting together the parts in the best possible order to get the desired result. In most planning of this kind, many of the various operations and processes fall into similar groups. Activities that require the same or related skills and knowledge should be grouped together as a natural organizational unit. However, some kinds of work fit into more than one group with equal facility, so in these instances, you have to use your best judgment as to where to put them.

By this planning, you have arrived at a tentative organizational pattern. Each grouping of related activities is a probable unit in the new structure. As a whole, they comprise all of the kinds of work required to meet the objective. Because you have to think of the entire operation as well as its parts,

you must study the relationships between each of the groupings. Here, again, two heads are better than one. This is a
good time to discuss your preliminary layout with others to
supplement your own judgment. In such discussions, it is wise
to limit the problem to the work itself: the operations, tasks,
and processes that logically go together, avoiding the question
of who does what.

By this time, you should be able to put your groupings on
paper in the form of a chart. This helps to clarify the relationships between the functions and encourages questions
about how the proposed organization will work. Changes can
be easily made to avoid trouble spots or to secure better flow
of work from one unit to another. The more questions that can
be raised and answered at this point, the better.

Utilizing present resources

The groupings form the plan of organization as you would
like to see it, but you have to consider the practical aspects
of working with the physical resources and people that you
have. Questions of space, equipment, and facilities arise. What
you would like to have might not be available. Before you can
put your plan into action, you have to find out if these
items can be secured. If not, further modification has to be
made.

You should review the abilities and personalities of the work
force in a similar way. "Do you have the skills and knowledge
to staff each group adequately? Are there enough competent
workmen of each kind? Will they work together happily and
productively? Will you have to train or retrain some of them?
Will hiring be necessary? Do you have competent supervisors
for each group? Will all current employees qualify for the
jobs necessary in the proposed setup? Will there be any em-

ployees left who should be transferred? Do you have any individuals who do not fit into the new pattern? What will you do with them?"

It was suggested that you discuss your tentative organizational plan with others before you arrive at the staffing stage. Now you are considering the utilization of people, so you must be careful. If members of a work force learn a reorganization is contemplated, they are likely to be concerned about what will happen to them. Rumors are bound to circulate, and morale may be seriously affected. Under these circumstances, it is unwise to permit your preliminary personnel planning to become widely known. The final decisions are seldom the same as the tentative proposals made while you are working out the structure and its staffing. To prevent disquieting rumors, most executives confine discussions of personnel changes to their supervisors and the staff specialists who can be of help. Sound personnel management also indicates that the work force should be told as a group that a reorganization is proposed and the natural fears about job security allayed if workers begin to be upset by the usual wild rumors.

Making final adjustments

When you attempt to fit the human and material resources into your organizational structure, you are going to have to make some adjustments. This should not be an occasion for arguments, frustrations, or temper displays. The experienced organizer realizes an ideal structure is seldom possible. Sound management realistically expects the natural compromises necessary for democratic supervision and effective human relations. Fitting the pattern of organization to the conditions as you find them is a perfectly normal procedure, and it is necessary if the plan is to function efficiently.

Trying out the plan

A reorganization is nothing more than a plan unless it is put into effect. Frequently it can be done on a trial basis to test its effectiveness and make additional modifications to improve it. The tryout must be well planned so everyone involved fully understands his part in the new setup. During this period, the organizer should be free to observe what happens, to identify any trouble and to make sure employees are actually doing what they are supposed to do. After the trial period, he should sit down with his advisory group to analyze the results and secure agreement on the desirability of any further adjustments before final installation.

In other instances, it is not feasible to have a tryout, so the new organizational pattern has to be put in operation as it was conceived. This means taking a calculated management risk but a perfectly normal one based upon good planning and a sound decision. Furthermore, the completeness with which the installation of the new pattern is planned will tend to ensure its success. The first few days or weeks of operating can be considered as a trial period to eliminate trouble spots and make final modification.

EFFECTS OF POOR ORGANIZATION

Whenever people combine their efforts to accomplish a common purpose, some of the effort must be organized. Otherwise, the people may be working at cross-purposes with each other, and the total result will be less than the sum of the individual activities. As mentioned previously, any plan to organize group activities, even an obviously inadequate one, will result in a greater output than the workers could produce individually. And finally, the better an operation is organized, the more efficiently it will be performed.

A poorly organized activity, then, fails to give the degree of efficiency that could be achieved under a better plan. These effects are important to managers because they indicate a disorganized condition that merits correction. Some of the more apparent signals are worth noting.

Lack of control

A supervisor seldom fails to recognize when his working conditions get out of control. There is confusion, wasted time and effort, and ineffective teamwork. It is difficult to find out what is going on; work reports are late, inaccurate, or incomplete; and problems multiply. Although these conditions are not always just a result of poor organization, they reflect a need for immediate correction that often requires a better organizational setup.

Decentralization

In an organization where relationships are not clearly defined or activities are incorrectly grouped, there is a natural tendency for subordinate units to assume authority and responsibilities that are not formally assigned to them. They are often forced to make decisions because it is the only way to get the work accomplished. This decentralizes authority to lower echelons and may result in a situation where higher management levels are not aware of what is happening. It breaks the chain of command, and none of the management functions operate effectively.

Autonomous action

In a closely related situation, when organizational relationships are poorly defined, a subordinate supervisor may take complete charge and run his operation to suit himself. If positive direction is lacking, there is a strong likelihood that this will happen. Strong-willed individuals tend to become "empire builders" under this condition. It further complicates the problem because the relationships become even more disorganized. Good management gives prompt attention to any indication of autonomous action.

Misunderstandings

The more clearly relations between organizational units are defined and understood, the less chance there is for misunderstandings between the persons involved. Conversely, a poor organization opens the way to overlapping of responsibility, differences of opinion, and arguments. Even in the best-organized companies, the complexity of work makes full communication difficult; but, any increase in misunderstanding between operating units should be a signal to examine the organizational structure.

Strain between headquarters and field offices

In any large organization, the relationships, channels, and line of command between the upper and lower levels must be kept clear. This can be ensured only with the highest type of organizational planning. Strained relationships are particularly likely to develop between headquarters and field offices because of geographical separation and differences in approach to problems of mutual interest. Lack of agreement on purpose, policy, authority, timing, procedures, or controls can seriously impede progress. Sound organizational planning eliminates or minimizes these sources of inefficiency.

BENEFITS OF SOUND ORGANIZATION

If group effort becomes more productive when it is well organized, it follows that its primary benefit is more efficient operations. Although this is perfectly true, such a statement is so general that it is somewhat meaningless. Therefore, here are a few more specific ways in which efficiency can be improved.

Improved communications

During the last few years, more attention has been given to achieving better management communication. Because of their size, many companies have had to rely on "official channels" to a considerable extent for flow of information upward and downward. For all practical purposes, these channels are defined by the structure of the organization. Thus, even within a single plant or office, official communication is facilitated by clearly defined lines of authority.

Official channels do not, however, provide for an easy flow of information horizontally. Much essential communication is authorized between organizational segments on similar levels in both written and oral form. Telephones save time and expense if it is possible to identify the unit that can supply the needed information. Personal contacts are invaluable for getting "the whole story." A clear definition of functional responsibility is of great help to anyone searching for a source of information. In fact, it is common practice to refer to an organizational chart or manual to identify correct sources.

One further aspect of communication is the emphasis placed by organization analysts on reducing the number of "layers" of supervision. The more levels between top management and the work force, the greater the difficulties of communication. The same thing is true within a single division or even a section. Sears Roebuck and Co. has had successful results by eliminating unnecessary layers of management and thus "flattening" the organizational structure. The flow of information is facilitated, and the overhead cost of management and supervision is minimized.

Better utilization of material

The careful analysis that precedes organizational decisions takes into account the material resources required to make the plan work successfully. As tasks, processes, and ·activities are studied to discover the most effective grouping, careful attention should be given to physical requirements. The selection of appropriate tools and equipment; the provision of adequate space, heat, light, and power; and the layout of operations are all factors that should be considered thoughtfully to obtain maximum utilization.

Economical use of manpower

In a similar way, and possibly to an even greater degree, organizational planning focuses attention on staffing. The importance of the human factor was mentioned earlier. Sound organization not only permits operating with a minimum number of employees but also achieves further economy by increasing the efficiency of their group efforts. This is so basic to the whole theory of organization that it is unnecessary to do more than point it out.

Correct management decisions

Chapter 3 went into the matter of thinking through how to come up with good answers when they are needed. It was pointed out that the quality of the decision depended largely on getting the pertinent facts. In a well-organized operation, this information is available and can be obtained readily when needed. Careful definition of relationships assists in the analysis of difficulties and makes it easier to identify the persons who can contribute most to the solution.

These conditions obviously help to improve the quality of decisions. It is equally apparent that they facilitate the decision-making process so answers are forthcoming when needed. Another effect is to reduce the number of serious operating problems to be resolved. The better the relations between units, the fewer opportunities there are for trouble. When difficulties do arise, management officials have more time to get the facts and come up with sound decisions.

RESPONSIBILITY FOR STRUCTURE

The theory of the organization process and its application to the work situation have been discussed in this and the preceding chapters. The implication throughout has been that supervisors and executives are responsible for determining the structure of the units under their direction. This is based on the assumption that the manager of an operation knows more about how it should be organized than anyone else. Although such an assumption is valid in theory, it is not always entirely true in practice.

Possibly a more correct statement might be that you, as an operating official, know more about your people, processes, equipment, and working conditions than anyone else. All such information is essential to organizational planning, but it is also possible that there are significant aspects of the operation that escape your notice. Furthermore, unless you have previously had an opportunity to think through what is involved in organizing an activity, you may lack competence in this direction.

Recognizing your basic responsibility to maintain an effective organizational structure for your unit, here is a brief review of the responsibilities of other persons who can assist you in, or who influence, the structure of your operations.

The management office

In large organizations, there is almost always a staff office with specific responsibility for management improvements. In smaller companies, a single management engineer may carry out these duties. Organization and methods examiners may be used to survey the structure of every segment of the establishment and recommend changes for greater efficiency. Sometimes supervisors resent these specialists intruding into their departments. They fear the effects of upset working conditions that are bound to follow, and they hate to have the old pattern changed.

Although this attitude is understandable, it is unfortunate. Managers actually should welcome any opportunity for skilled analysts to review operations because their task of improving work efficiency coincides exactly with the manager's own objective. Here is a chance to use skilled assistance to improve organization and make one's own job less onerous. It makes good sense to work closely with these people so the best possible structure is achieved jointly.

The job evaluation staff

Another group of specialists is concerned with job classification and wages. Their responsibility is to make sure that as far as possible employees receive equal pay for equal work. They also ascertain that the technical provisions of the labor contract are carried out with respect to pay matters.

This work is closely connected with the organizational structure of your unit. In the first place, the position an employee occupies in the organization has a great deal to do with his duties and responsibilities and, hence, with the rating of his job. Unless the nature of the work and its relation to other jobs is clearly defined, the person who classifies positions may find his audit does not justify the assigned level. This would seriously affect the existing structure.

Secondly, the pattern of organization affects the job level. There is a normal alignment of grade levels descending from the top to the bottom. The analyst must try to preserve this relationship. The more efficiently the operation is organized, the easier it is to preserve a sound job alignment.

Finally, the classification of jobs should be an essential factor in planning your structure, so it is desirable to secure technical assistance from these specialists during the planning stage. They can be helpful in defining job relationships and ensuring that no classification difficulties arise after an organizational change is made.

Higher echelons

Constantly changing conditions result in frequent changes of purpose. There are always many factors shaping policy. They frequently result in decisions on fund allocation or strength control. Whenever a higher echelon determines that a change is necessary, the impact of the decision is felt throughout the subordinate segments of the organization. These situations should be expected and adjusted to without reluctance because they are normal in any large enterprise.

Organizational structures are sure to be affected whenever any drastic changes occur in funds or personnel. In some instances, standard "Tables of Organization" are prescribed, establishing limits to the number of employees in each grade. Each such table represents a higher level management decision on the number of people necessary to carry out the operation. Ordinarily, these tables furnish a valuable standard to gauge the efficiency of your unit. If you have serious difficulty in getting the job done with the number of persons allowed, you should immediately review your layout, methods and organizational pattern to find out what could be wrong.

SUMMARY

The study of the organization process has clearly indicated that it is far more than a mere theory of management. It determines to a large degree how efficiently and economically work assignments are carried out. Alvin Brown pointed out in his book *Organization of Industry* [2] that often there is little difference in the fundamental ability of the successful and the unsuccessful manager. The determining factor may be only a small degree of better planning, sounder decision, careful checkup. The man who becomes known as an effective organizer has usually established a reputation as a competent manager.

[2] Alvin Brown, *Organization of Industry,* Prentice-Hall, Inc., Englewood Cliffs, N. J., 1947, p. 350.

7

Directing Operations

To maintain correct perspective, it should be recalled that this study of job management was approached from the point of view of its three broad aspects: planning, taking executive action and controlling. These three phases correspond exactly to the five processes of management if one considers the middle one, executive action, as representing what is done in organizing, directing, and coordinating the work.

This does not mean executives do all their planning at one time, execute the plans, and finally check on the results. Rather it means that persons who are responsible for work operations are continuously planning and replanning, giving directions to secure well-coordinated action in their part of the organization, and inspecting the work to be sure it is under control. Yet, the three aspects are usually considered in this order because each part of the job must be planned before action can be taken and, only after work is under way, can the results be checked. To tie these ideas together, they are given here in their proper place in relation to the three phases of management:

Planning	1. Determines *purpose*
	2. *Decides* what, how, when, by whom, and where
Executive	1. Sets up working *organization*
Action	2. *Directs* action to secure desired results
	3. *Coordinates* actions for greatest effectiveness
Control	1. *Checks* on results through inspection
	2. Uses quantity and quality *controls*

At this point it is necessary to go into methods of directing work operations. For the purposes of the discussion, the term "directing" is defined as communicating your decisions and those of higher management to your immediate subordinates. The word "subordinate" here, as elsewhere in the text, does not imply inferiority. It is used to identify those who report directly to you or are under your direction. They, in turn, may transmit the information to others who report to them.

NATURE OF THE PROCESS

This brief review high lights the management official's responsibility to get the work under way, to initiate action, and to supply information to his people. When you give directions, you are communicating downward in the organization. Communication is effective only to the degree that it conveys the meaning you intend: the results you get from members of your work force depend primarily on whether or not they understand what you want. Thus, the process of directing is equally as important as any of the others in achieving good job management.

Relation to delegation

It was already pointed out how it becomes necessary in the process of organizing an activity to subdivide the many operations and assign them to employees. By this delegation, you place specific responsibilities on your subordinates to carry out these duties for you. You, too, have been delegated broad responsibility, and commensurate authority, by higher authority to see that certain objectives are attained. Because you cannot accomplish this through your own personal efforts, you must delegate appropriate parts of the work to others. They, in turn, become responsible for discharging their part of the total task. They assume a delegated responsibility to accomplish the assignment; you continue to carry a retained responsibility to see they perform their parts satisfactorily.

This process is always rather formal and recorded in functional statements and job descriptions. Primarily, it spells out what is required, rather than how or why it is done. It includes giving the employee the authority he needs to discharge the responsibility. It resembles directing because it is also downward communication.

Ordinarily, giving directions is a far less formal matter. Frequently they are oral, but if they are written, they are seldom made a matter of official record even though they may be permanent. They also tend to cover the how and why of the assignment more thoroughly, including instructions and explanations. In this sense, job instruction becomes a part of the directing function.

Relation to authority

It is an axiom of management that an executive or supervisor, by virtue of his position, has the authority to require subordinates to comply with his delegations or directions. This does not imply you must always resort to authority to secure compliance. Just because one has authority is no reason to flaunt it. In fact, most successful managers seldom have to use it because everyone knows and respects it. There are times, however, such as refusal to obey, failure to carry out directions, or emergencies requiring immediate action when one must exercise authority.

Authority comes to you by delegation from your immediate supervisor, and the nature and extent should be stated in your job description. Sometimes this is lacking. In any event, you should be sure you thoroughly understand how far you can go in directing others. The more clearly your scope of authority can be defined, the better for all concerned. In redelegation to those below you, you should be equally careful to secure complete understanding.

Everyone has known of situations where someone exceeded his authority. This always brings unpleasant results. The best way to avoid such trouble is to know the extent of your authority. Beyond this, your own good judgment will tell you when and how it is to be used. It is also well to keep in mind that the right to direct may be applied only to those who report to you directly; you weaken the position of a subordinate supervisor by giving directions to his workers. And, of course, you would never direct employees outside of your own organizational segment.

TYPES OF DIRECTING

Orders

There is constant reference in the military to the word "command." Historically, the military have used "orders" to give directions. Accompanying this is the concept of unquestioned, and unquestioning, obedience to the command, which, in turn, is based on the oath of service. The strong emphasis on rank in military organizations is an expression of this reliance on authority.

In the business world, employees cannot, and should not, be managed in a similar manner. Today, the word "boss" takes on a paternalistic meaning and often implies a high degree of respect and friendliness. This contrasts sharply with its former usage, referring to a "bossy" person who demanded obedience and based his claim to leadership on force and fear. Few such supervisors remain today.

Most employees resent being ordered to do something. Although they may comply in either case, they usually respond willingly to a courteous request but grudgingly to a command. To secure wholehearted cooperation, management officials have learned to use orders sparingly, only in those few situations where the use of authority is necessary.

Although you seldom resort to orders in the sense of commands to direct operations, you do use this term frequently in many appropriate situations. Usually the term means work orders of some familiar pattern, which are accepted and complied with as routine communications. If the orders involve new or unusual circumstances, they are nearly always accompanied by supplementary directions.

Instructions and explanations

A prevalent trend in current supervisor-employee relations is toward the teamwork idea. In a sense, the only reason to have management officials is to assist their subordinates to get the work accomplished efficiently. It is not unusual to find situations in industry where labor has as much, if not more, to say about working conditions than the employer. Negotiations with organized employee groups are required under provisions of labor law.

From this point of view, then, directing workers becomes a cooperative effort to secure complete understanding of what is required, and the necessity for ordering subordinates to do their work automatically disappears. Instead, employees meet with their supervisor for instructions and explanations. Although the process is still essentially downward communication there is an opportunity for questions and comments in both directions.

Here, the word "instruction" means to furnish employees the information needed to carry out an assignment. This is in contrast to the use of the term as planned job training or the giving of "instruction." In the former sense, directions are a normal part of your day-to-day job relations with your employees. The instruction should include more than just what to do. It should also state how the work is to be done, who is to do it, where it can be done best, and when it is needed.

Explanations usually go one step beyond instructions, telling the workers why the assignment is necessary. Giving a reason is an important incentive; everyone likes to know why he is being asked to do something. Further, it gives those concerned the opportunity to ask questions or make suggestions on how the work can be facilitated.

The situation

A school of thought that is widely followed today is, "Let the situation give the order." Actually, it makes real sense. Simply stated, it means pointing out to workers all of the factors in the work situation that make a desired action necessary. When they understand the logic behind the order, they comply more willingly. There is less need to resort to authority, give orders, or force action. Clever supervisors use this method to get employees to set their own directions at work.

Similarly, it is not unusual for leaders to indicate what they want done by the example they set. In many situations, actions speak louder than words. If you want your employees to handle a certain part with particular care, you can demonstrate this by your own actions. If you want them to wear safety shoes for a particular operation, you can insist on putting on a pair yourself when you go into that situation. Most people are imitative and so this indirect method is effective.

GIVING DIRECTIONS

Although you can effectively supplement your work direction by showing how you want work performed, you must still rely mainly on words. Yet, even in simple situations, everyone has experienced difficulty in getting people to understand fully what is meant. Difficulties in verbal communication come about for several reasons:

Words have different meanings for different people.
The words may be used incorrectly.
They may not be written or heard clearly.
They may arouse resentment or antagonism.
They may not adequately convey full meaning.

Oral directions

By far, the majority of directions are spoken; you tell people what to do and how to do it. There are several ways to give this kind of instructions to an individual. They are important enough to deserve a brief review:

By order: "Sign this letter."

May be necessary in some situations, such as deadlines or emergencies
Secures quick compliance
Tends to be harsh
Is often resented by workers
Is used cautiously by most supervisors

By request: "Will you please sign this letter?"

Is the most common method
Is less harsh than command
Assumes a willingness to comply
Makes receiver feel less subservient

By suggestion (implied order): "This letter should be signed promptly."

Is used occasionally if employee thoroughly understands what to do
May be misunderstood
May be disregarded

This analysis makes it clear that you have a choice in the way you give directions to an individual worker, and this means you have to use judgment in each instance. Should you order, request, or suggest? Each method is appropriate under certain circumstances. Too many supervisors fail to realize that they can make their spoken directions more effective by simply using the form that best suits each situation.

In the first place, people are different. The more you understand each individual and the way he is likely to react to your words, the better you can phrase your directions to secure his willing cooperation. For instance, good judgment would lead you to use a slightly different approach with an older employee, a highly nervous or sensitive person, a chronic objector, or a high-ranking scientist.

Working conditions also influence what you say. Although it is desirable to have the situation give the order, it is not always possible. The way you give directions to people will vary with the circumstances. You would use quite different methods in a case of immediate danger, in assigning a simple task, in a hazardous situation, in striving for improved methods, in avoiding possible anger, or in a situation where speed is important. Fitting your words to the situation can help make your directions far more effective.

Much of what has been said on directing individuals also applies to groups. Certainly you will want to plan carefully to be sure your presentation arouses interest, secures attention, and is fully understood. Here, you have an opportunity to arrange the situation so everyone can see and hear you.

Often you meet your people in a staff meeting, so you can plan much of what you will say and do in advance. You can even predict to some degree the questions that will be asked and how to answer them, the kind of comments that will come from various individuals, the nature of the group's first reaction, and the change of attitudes you will want to bring about.

In some instances, you may have to call a group of employees together briefly and informally for specific directions. This might occur if you discover a general misunderstanding of previous directions that should be corrected immediately. Although you do not have an opportunity to plan extensively what you will say, you still need to make a quick mental review of how you are going to make your remarks most effective. Unless you do, you may cause further confusion.

Some of the obstacles in giving directions orally are worth noting. They represent rather common faults but ones that anyone can correct if he makes the effort. They are pitfalls to be avoided.

Haziness

Lack of care in choice of words
"Take care of the books" can mean bookkeeping or library work
Failure to give complete information
"Transfer those files I want moved."

Hurry and pressure

Pushing for hasty action
"Get rid of that man immediately!"
Using unnecessary force
"Your job depends on this."

Complex phrasing

Talking too fast
"Just what did the boy say?"
Using unfamiliar words
"Do you understand?" "Oh sure!"

Too much at one time

Giving prolonged instructions
Discussing several unrelated subjects

Failure to give reasons

Providing no real incentive
Encouraging resistance to the change

Attention to these points will help you achieve effective oral direction of the work, and persistence will result in better habits of speech for any occasion. A few other common-sense hints that will improve oral directions are:

Know exactly what you want to say before you start talking.
Speak slowly and loudly enough to be heard.

Avoid telling too much at one time.

Explain what you mean if you have to use unfamiliar terms.

Have the directions repeated back to you.

A simple illustration, probably familiar to everyone, may help crystallize the difference between good and bad oral directions:

Motorist: (Lost and in a hurry to get to Cobb's Corners) Pardon me. Can you tell me how to get to Cobb's Corners?

Stranger No. 1: Well, now let's see, that's on Route 14, ain't it?

Stranger No. 2: Did you say Cobb's Corners? That's about six miles north of Old Church.

Stranger No. 1: That's right, friend, you turn around and go back to the crossroads. It's only a couple of miles from there.

Motorist: Can I make a U turn here?

Stranger No. 1: No, you have to go on up a couple of blocks and turn on Fourth Street.

Stranger No. 2: Wouldn't it be better for him to turn on Hogan's Alley?

Motorist: Thank you! I guess I can find it.

Strangers Nos. 1 and 2: Sure, you can't miss it.

Contrast that example with the kind of reply that might have been given:

"Yes, indeed. You have to go back a few miles; you are now on Main Street headed east. Go ahead two blocks to the first stop light, then turn right one block and right again on Hyatt Street. Keep on Hyatt Street for about one mile to Old Church. There's a direction sign on the right side of the road, and the church is on the left. Turn right there on Route 14 and go north six miles, that will take you to Cobb's Corners. Here, I sketched the route on this card. Do you want to repeat the directions back to me to be sure they're clear to you?"

Written directions

Oral directions were discussed in considerable detail because they are used continually and because many of the same points also apply to written directions. Literally whole libraries of books have been published on the subject of written communication. In addition to a wealth of texts on effective writing, there are also manuals on correspondence and on preparation of instructional materials. All of these can be helpful if you can find time to read and study them and have the desire to use them. Here, the discussion will be limited to a few practical aspects of the subject.

Nearly all written directions fall into one of three types. First, there are the broad, general instructions that are typed or printed and posted on bulletin boards for the instruction of all employees. They are not all necessarily directions; some may be merely announcements. However, if they involve changes of purpose or policy, work standards, safety, or other measures affecting operations, they represent management direction in the sense used in the preceding text.

A second type is represented by the rules, regulations, instructions, or operating procedures that are given to employees for their guidance. They may apply to the entire work force, only to employees engaged in a particular type of operation, or to a single worker. They are usually of a much more specific nature than those posted for general information, but often they also are posted for ready reference. These directions conserve the time of management officials by eliminating the need for frequent oral repetition. People do forget and become confused. The printed word helps to keep them clear.

The last type is known as the directive. This is a communication on a specific subject addressed to a particular person or group. It sets forth the executive action required and demands compliance, and usually requires an answer. It may be either formal correspondence or just a handwritten note to an employee. As with the other written methods, it may be used to supplement oral directions or vice versa.

RECEIVING DIRECTIONS

Management officials not only direct the work efforts of the employees who report to them, they also receive directions from above. Both are important aspects of the directing process, and they are interdependent in two ways. First, if your supervisor fails to give you clear, complete, and timely directions, you cannot transmit them effectively to your subordinates. Secondly, because you sometimes suffer as the recipient of inadequate instructions, you can put yourself in the position of your own employees when you fail to give them clear directions.

Guidance from management is in either oral or written form or both. Unless you understand it completely, full communication cannot be effected. Because your supervisor is a busy person with normal human susceptibility to err, at times he will fail to make his meaning clear. Actually, some of the responsibility for lack of understanding may be yours, but regardless of the cause, until you know what is wanted, you cannot accomplish it.

These situations pose some difficult problems, particularly if you are directed to make a drastic change. When you first hear or read the directions, they may seem quite clear. Later, when you have had a chance to mull over the various aspects of the matter, you may discover areas of uncertainty and questions will arise. You need more direction.

More frequently you might not grasp the whole story when

it is first presented. Doubts arise; your natural resistance to change asserts itself; or you jump to the conclusion that "it won't work." Permitting yourself the luxury of such an attitude makes it more difficult to grasp the full meaning because your mind is at least partially closed and the channel of communication is blocked.

What can you do to open up your "receiving set" for directions coming to you? Probably the first step is to get yourself in a receptive mood. The person giving the directions thinks there is a valid reason for giving them. You can search for that reason; look for the benefit to be derived and consciously strive to keep an open mind. This implies you should listen or read attentively.

Normally, provision is made for you to discuss directions in a conference situation with your immediate superior or any others concerned, such as interested technicians. This is your chance to ask the questions that will clear up any points you do not understand and fill in possible omissions. A pad of paper and pencil are helpful so you can jot down questions that flash through your mind, beginning with the old stand-bys: who, how, where, when, and why? It is far better to ask an unnecessary or even a silly question, than to fail to understand completely. By paying careful attention to points raised by other persons you may see implications you would otherwise fail to note.

Except in the most familiar matters, normally further problems arise as you carry out the directions. If you are to accomplish the objective efficiently, these questions must also be answered. To do so, you may have to go back to your supervisor for further explanation, question others involved in the operation, or talk with technicians who are informed about the situation. If you fail to find out exactly what is expected, you must accept the full responsibility if something goes wrong.

SOME PERSONNEL MANAGEMENT IMPLICATIONS

It is apparent that any organized effort must be competently directed to operate efficiently. Management officials can plan carefully, set up a sound organizational structure, and still fail to reach the goal if clear direction is not provided. Therefore, direction is a primary link in the chain of essential management processes. Because it is so fundamental, it is closely related to some aspects of personnel management.

Employee training

It was mentioned earlier that giving *instructions* is closely related to giving *instruction* in the sense of planned training. Both are communication; both are used to inform the work force about operations. Considering both activities as part of the directing function does not alter the meaning of either. Actually, there is a step-by-step gradation from a carefully planned training program of several weeks' duration, to less formal and extensive job training, on down to the casual remark that directs an individual employee to do a task a certain way. Even such specialized activities as executive development, supervisor training programs, and on-the-job rotational training assignments are devices providing direction to the employees concerned.

Performance evaluation

In both industry and government there is currently a heavy emphasis on appraisal of the work performance of employees at all levels. Under the Performance Rating Act of 1950, all Federal employees must have their job performances appraised and rated by a system approved by the Civil Service Commission. Group appraisal plans similar to that described by Virgil Rowland and used in the Detroit Edison Co.[1] are quite popular. Undoubtedly, there are many direct and indirect benefits from such systems, but some companies think they are too time consuming and that satisfactory appraisals can be secured through more simple and economical means. The purpose of these plans is to improve job competence and supervisor-employee relations more than to secure a rating.

Emphasis, then, shifts from the evaluation itself to the actions that follow. A careful review of the accomplishments of an employee almost invariably brings to light aspects of his work that could be improved. Here, a supervisor must often give additional directions, instructions, or explanations. When this happens, the directing process is being used.

Consultative management

Many companies are experimenting with so-called Junior Boards to identify, develop, and utilize the latent capacities of employees. Usually such a plan starts with the selection of a small group of younger employees who have demonstrated management potential. They meet regularly to discuss problems of current importance and make recommendations for their solution. After six months or a year, the members of the group appraise each other. These appraisals are used as a basis to change the composition of the group and create opportunities for new members. Normally about half of the

[1] Virgil K. Rowland, Case XXXVII, The Detroit Edison Company in "The Development of Executive Talent," American Management Association, 1952, p. 393.

Also Report 4, Series 1, Human Relations Program, Institute for Social Research of University of Michigan by Floyd Mann and James Dent, 1954.

members stay on, and the vacancies are filled by selecting other promising persons. The most famous of these systems is used by McCormick & Co., Inc., of Baltimore.

There are many variations to this device, but all of them try to encourage growth in the management competence of the members so there will be an ample reserve of potential executives when needed. Another important outcome of these boards is that their recommendations are frequently adopted. When this happens, management officials have to direct the changes in operations. Again, the directing function is involved, not by the recommending group, but by the managers as a result of the suggestion.

SUMMARY

This description of directing the activities of an organization clearly points out the importance of the process. Planning, organizing, coordinating, and controlling of operations take place more often on higher levels than in the lower supervisory jobs. The reverse is true of directing. Lower-level supervisors spend most of their time directing the work of their employees. Department heads, on the other hand, do not have to do so because the people who report to them are carefully selected, experienced employees who do not need continuous direction. Even so, every executive directs the operations entrusted to him to the extent necessary, and every supervisor uses all of the management processes to some degree.

Directing work operations resembles driving an automobile in some ways. Before he takes the wheel, the driver makes sure the construction of the car is well *planned* and all its parts are *organized* to work together. Also he checks that he has his driver's license because it is his *authority* to drive. Satisfied on these points, he is ready to start; he must know how to get the motor turning over and also how to shift gears. Even if he knows where he wants to go, he will never reach his *objective* by spinning the wheels or stalling the motor. Of course, the driver could get there in low gear, but he would waste gas and probably overheat the motor. His progress would be costly and slow.

Once in high gear, he has to give constant attention to his *direction*. Sometimes it is necessary to change direction, so, to be safe, the driver slows down. The more abrupt the change, the more cautiously he approaches it. He may have to apply the brake. A good driver keeps his eyes on the road and his hands on the wheel. He *guides* the mechanism with a sure, smooth touch, always keeping in his own line of traffic and watching for road signs. He interprets these and communicates to the car by varying the amount of power to fit the situations. If the unexpected does happen, he does not lose his head; he keeps the car under firm *control*. In due time, the driver reaches his objective as planned, and the car is ready to continue on the next trip.

8

Coordinating Operations

To secure effective executive action from your employees, you must give attention to the relationship of each task, activity, or process with all of the others. You have planned your organization, policies, and procedures to accomplish your objective efficiently. When action starts, you want it to flow smoothly and harmoniously with as little friction, lost motion, or delay as possible. This coordination is an important function of management.

To state it a little differently, it has already been noted that:

1. Job planning goes on all the time; you have to look ahead and plan in advance to achieve the most effective results.

2. You are ready to take action as soon as you decide what is to be done, how it is to be done, and who is to do it; you exercise your authority as a manager by directing your organization in line with these decisions

3. All organized effort is teamwork and, as such, requires careful timing if you are to secure high productivity from the effort.

Coordination, then, is the term representing the actions you take to ensure that work flow is properly timed and all operations fit together smoothly. It deals with securing harmonious relationships between all aspects of the operation.

NATURE OF THE PROCESS

Harmony is a key word in understanding the meaning of coordination. Usually it is used in connection with music; the same is true of timing. The conductor of an orchestra plans his program, decides on the numbers, and organizes the disposition of brasses, woodwinds, strings, and percussion instruments. Now he is ready to direct the performance. Regardless of how highly skilled each player may be, the combined efforts would be completely ruined without effective coordination. If the first violinist plays Bach when the others begin Debussy, it is impossible to achieve harmony. It would be equally disastrous if the tuba came in on a solo reserved for the flute. Each individual contribution must be perfectly timed.

Just as the conductor must coordinate all the instruments, so the manager must secure timing and harmony in the productive efforts of his employees. A watch is another excellent example of coordination. Each part must be in perfect relationship with every other part in order to run efficiently. If the relationship is disturbed and timing is incorrect, the watch fails to serve its purpose.

Coordination of many operations is also extremely important in building a house. If floors are laid before the roof is put on, there is a possibility of heavy damage. Plastering must not precede wiring if there is to be any sort of economy; the plumber cannot be scheduled to put in the pipes, fixtures, and heating plant after the carpenters, plasterers, and painters have finished. In fact, the operations of every group of workmen must be coordinated with the rest to avoid work crews wasting time by waiting for the others.

The modern production-line technique is a striking illustration of good coordination. Each step is so minutely timed that every part reaches the exact spot where it is needed at the correct moment. This involves the distribution of workers and machines in such proportions that each product item or subassembly emerges in the right quantity when needed. It is easy to visualize how production would be affected if two right-front fenders came down to an automobile assembly line when a front and a rear were needed or if one red and one green door arrived for the same chassis.

These examples clearly show that the coordination of effort depends upon the degree of planning and organizing that goes into the work. It is equally apparent that each member of the team must have clear directions on his part in the total process, not only how he is to perform his tasks but also when he is to do this share in relation to the jobs being performed by other members of the team. Finally, a high degree of control is necessary if the result is to be satisfactory.

COORDINATING ACTIVITIES WITHIN YOUR UNIT

As the manager of your own unit, you have a continuing responsibility to see that the activities under your direction are properly synchronized. Like the other management processes, coordination of work is not something that can be achieved once and for all, needing no further attention. Changes in work are a normal result of changing markets, methods, or top-level decisions. They may be initiated on a national scale, by someone in a single plant, or by a foreman who thinks a change will be beneficial.

Because progress only results from change, you should view

each such situation as an opportunity to effect better coordination of the activities under your control. This requires a thoughtful study of what is happening, that is, a management analysis of how smoothly your part of the organization is functioning. Some of the more common directions in which you focus your attention follow.

Process analysis

This is concerned with the work methods and procedures used by the employee group as a whole. One of the most effective ways to size up your operations is simply to stand back and take a fresh look at them. Day-to-day activities keep you so deeply immersed in specific problems and details that you might "fail to see the forest for the trees."

The main drawback to this approach is that everyone has difficulty in disassociating himself, even temporarily, from the minor problems of the moment. It takes real effort to put these things out of your mind so you can consciously perceive what is going on. One way is to approach the work situation as though you were a stranger who had never seen it before. It is surprising how this sharpens your perception.

It is equally important to adopt a critical attitude toward what you are reviewing. The more questions you can ask yourself, the better. "Why does that requisition have to stay on Joe's desk for several hours? What does he do with it? Is it really necessary for him to handle it at all? Why is so much unfinished work waiting to be processed? Why is Section A so rushed when Section B is taking things easy? How long does it take for a piece of work to pass through the unit? Are there any unnecessary delays? Where do they occur? Why?"

Merely asking such questions may give you a better idea of whether the work is being processed smoothly and harmoniously. But if you want to improve internal coordination, you need to get the answers as well. This usually requires the help of the employees because they are the ones who are doing the work. They may have excellent ideas on how to secure better timing of work flow. Certainly their points of view should be considered.

Several special techniques have been devised to assist in the analysis of work processes. One of these is the process analysis chart which records every step in a process in detail on a special form. Each individual step is identified and studied to see if better coordination can be effected. Another is the work flow chart which diagrams exactly how an item of work gets from one place to another. Both are helpful. However, until a supervisor is experienced in the use of these devices, he usually gets better results by calling on the management technicians for their help. Working with them on process or work flow chart development and analysis is profitable experience. Brief descriptions of these two charts are given in Chapter 11.

Analysis of accomplishment

Even though process analysis is important in achieving coordination, it is also necessary to consider what is going on at individual work stations. Each employee, at any level in an organization, can either perform his work smoothly or drift into practices that substantially reduce efficiency. Reviewing the way an employee is getting his tasks done with him often uncovers situations where better coordination could be effected.

Such matters as the layout of the bench, desk, or machine area and the movements of the worker as he goes about the job are significant. Unnecessary reaching, bending, handling, or walking can slow down the timing of an operation. Clumsy or awkward work habits do the same. Both tire the worker prematurely and, thus, result in further delay. These aspects of coordination are also discussed in greater detail in Chapter 11.

Scheduling

Some attention to the scheduling of the operations is necessary to secure a smooth, harmonious flow of work. Normally, you expect each step of the work to be finished in reasonable time to meet the predetermined goals. Often this timing is fixed by setting a deadline or target date. In many production plants, job tickets with this information accompany the work in process to act as a control on the time allowance for various operations.

Scheduling of work is, of course, a part of production planning by which coordination can be effected. Many activities must be conducted under tight time limitations. The product, whether a paper, a part, or merely an oral report, must be ready when needed. With the exception of some types of protracted scientific research, more and more work processes are being scheduled to secure coordination.

Corrective or preventive actions

If a job order is not completed on time, if a production line gets snarled up, or if a case drags on without solution, you, as a manager, have to do something about it. Your first concern is to correct the trouble and get work moving smoothly again. In these instances, the desired coordination was not secured, and you want to get operations back on schedule as soon as possible.

However, coordination is essentially more a preventive than

corrective function. You plan your work flow, sequence of actions, assembly, and check points well in advance. You make process and performance analyses to ensure harmonious, efficient actions in the future and set schedules in advance to effect a coordination of the tasks involved. Thus, although the correction of present difficulties may involve the timing and harmony of activities, the primary purpose of coordination is to prevent friction and delays in the future.

COORDINATING WITH OTHER ACTIVITIES

A major aspect of maintaining smooth operations is your relationship with other activities in the organization and the various people you do business with. There is a natural tendency for these people to feel that what *they* are doing is the most important thing in the organization, the same as you feel about your contribution. The truth, of course, is that each part is essential to the proper functioning of the operation, and, in a sense, all parts are equally important. Unless you recognize this pride in accomplishment, you may not secure the full coordination of your efforts with those of others.

Normally, work flows through an organization from one part to another. When a holdup occurs, it usually affects more than one unit. If work comes in poorly prepared, coordination within the section may be adversely affected, and it may not get processed on schedule. This affects coordination with the receiving group.

To prevent such happenings, it is desirable to develop close, friendly, and cooperative relations with other units. The more you know about their operation, the better prepared you are for contingencies. This is advocating teamwork with other units as well as with your own. It is difficult to achieve coordination without cooperation, and you should keep in mind that cooperation works both ways: if you expect others to help you meet your schedule, you should be ready to put yourself to a little trouble occasionally to give them some assistance.

Everyone realizes that to get work accomplished, every single function of every organizational segment must be coordinated with all the activities related to it. This poses some difficult problems for anyone who has management responsibility. It is easy to recall instances where you have been delayed or your work held up because you could not get action from another work unit when you needed it. It may not be quite so easy to remember the times when you caused poor coordination. Although you cannot expect to be perfect, you can reduce your failures. They usually take place in three directions.

Coordinating with those to whom you report

The persons who direct your activities are key figures. Frequently they set your deadlines, give you production schedules, or establish the priority of assignments. They are often the source of work changes that can upset your carefully planned flow of work. Because this is so, it points again to the need to keep in close contact with your superior. You must make sure you get needed information as early as possible. If your operations are to be well coordinated, you must understand clearly what is expected of your unit and when.

There is another side to this situation. One of the major responsibilities of your superior is to secure coordination of the various operations under his direction. You must be certain he is informed about your total work situation, any major problems that disturb your scheduling, and particularly any situation that interferes with proper coordination of your work with other operations.

Coordinating with related work units

Relationships with other work units were discussed to emphasize the need for cooperation with the people involved. It was pointed out that it pays to maintain close contacts with the units from which you get work as well as those to which you send work. In addition, there are a few other hints that many management officials have found helpful:

Advise others of any changes in your work situation that might affect coordination.

Be as sure as you can that the supplies and equipment you need are available so your operation will meet its deadlines.

When necessary, adjust your work schedules as much as possible to meet the needs of the other unit.

Keep your temper when you hit a rough spot.

Coordinating with staff units

It is not unusual for staff specialists to be sent into your sections from time to time to make special studies. These visits often give rise to problems because of possible interference with normal operations. The finance officer may ask for data regarding contemplated repairs, new equipment, or budget estimates. The management office may be directed to make a survey of your organization or work methods. The personnel office may have to audit all the jobs or secure data to coordinate your manpower needs with the remainder of the organization.

In each case, some of your time is taken up and possibly that of your subordinates. The ensuing delay may throw your schedule off unless you take prompt steps to prevent it. Normally, you get advance notice of such activities, so you can take them into consideration in planning your work. Furthermore, staff specialists realize there is a possibility of interfering with work accomplishment and are careful to keep it to a minimum. In emergencies, it is appropriate to request postponement of a survey.

The brighter side of this picture is that these same specialists can be very helpful to you. Coordination of your work internally and with other activities is sometimes difficult. If you are not able to get a satisfactory answer after reasonable study and effort, it is advantageous to call on appropriate staff specialists for help. That is what they are for. You should never feel that it is a confession of weakness to request their technical services if they can assist you in securing better management. When you do ask for their help, you should keep in mind that they have other commitments and you will have to coordinate the timing of the service with their work schedule and your own.

TEAMWORK

Several references have been made to the necessity for teamwork. This is so closely interwoven with coordination that it deserves special attention.

All organized effort requires that people work together to get something accomplished. But, people do not always work *together*. Five men pulling on a rope to move a piece of heavy timber will not even budge it if they each pull at a different time. They can exert tremendous strength and tire themselves out completely with no effective result. What a difference when their efforts are coordinated! Pulling together as a team makes the task easier for everyone, and the work gets done quickly to the full satisfaction of all concerned.

This illustration is so simple that you might be inclined to pass it off, thinking, "So what!" But if you consider it, you can see the parallel to situations you face from time to time. There are numerous instances where people are not pulling together. In each case, the efforts of the team are uncoordinated. The wise manager is alert to any evidences of friction because they are symptoms that his people are not getting along together. He knows that coordination can be achieved only with smooth harmonious relationships.

There is increasing emphasis in management literature on this matter of human relations. A great deal of scientific research is being conducted to give fuller understanding of the complexities involved. Strong indications that human relations is one of the main factors in efficiency of work situations are coming out of these studies and experiments. Only when your employees get along together as a smoothly functioning team, can you secure the harmony needed for economical accomplishment.

It is not always eays to achieve this condition. People differ markedly in their interests, behavior, language, senses of humor, and consideration of others. It is easy for minor frictions to grow into major antagonisms. Real teamwork cannot exist if team members are at odds with one another. Supervisors and executives find it constantly necessary to apply the lubricant of sound personnel management to keep friction between people minimized.

Although everything a supervisor says or does affects his subordinates, there are a few guides that have helped others create and maintain a spirit of teamwork. They may be expressed as follows:

1. Develop a consistent attitude of fairness, friendliness, and firmness.

2. Establish and adhere to reasonable standards of accomplishment.

3. Plan work processes and work flow carefully.

4. Maintain working conditions at an optimum level.

5. Set an example of enthusiasm and optimism.

6. Commend individuals and groups for good teamwork.

7. Take prompt action to correct misunderstandings between subordinates.

SUMMARY

Everyone would agree that his job is easier when things move smoothly. You have a real personal interest, then, to see that your operations are well coordinated. Productivity is augmented to the degree that you achieve harmony, teamwork, and proper timing of activities.

This does not mean you should not welcome any change that will be an improvement. You cannot afford to bask in complacency or adopt the attitude that everything is good enough as it is. It would be fatal to the career of any management official to try merely to preserve the status quo. Because change is bound to occur, your problems of coordination are always with you.

It should be equally clear that you do not "coordinate" apart from the other management processes. Careful planning, sound organization, and clear directions all contribute to a smooth operation, yet, lack of harmony and teamwork can spoil your plans and upset your organization. You cannot depend on any one of the management processes for success. They are all interdependent and interfunctioning parts of the management cycle.

PART FOUR

Management Control

The third phase in the management cycle is to maintain sufficient control to be certain the purposes of the business are being attained efficiently. In the management sense, control means securing adequate information about the progress and results of the executive actions, interpreting these facts, and taking necessary corrective or preventive measures. It leads directly into replanning and, thus, starts the cycle anew.

9

Controlling Work Activities

The previous chapters analyzed the ways in which a manager sets up his goals, decides on the means to accomplish these purposes, and organizes his resources to take the necessary actions. Once the wheels start to turn, the question arises as to the *results* of these decisions and actions. Unless an answer is forthcoming, no one can be sure of what is happening, so control methods are designed to supply the needed information.

If all the people you employed were perfect, there would be no need for controls because everything would work out according to plan. But everyone makes mistakes from time to time. You might forget or fail to take action. You might make a bad decision. You might lose your temper. These conditions occur occasionally and are a definite part of every business situation. No one expects you to be perfect, but, on the other hand, you are expected to avoid making unnecessary errors.

Recognition of human imperfection is one reason why business, industry, and government have shown such great interest in the study of management. As you understand the principles involved and develop skill in applying them to actual work situations, you reduce the number of mistakes you might otherwise make. Because you can never achieve perfection, it is necessary to exercise control to find out what has gone wrong and to correct it. In addition, you should try to plan your control system to prevent errors from occurring.

GENERAL NATURE OF THE PROCESS

If management officials are to accomplish this, they must maintain a fairly close check on what is happening. In large organizations this is a difficult task. Adequate control depends upon a flow of significant, accurate, and timely information going up, down, and across. This process deals with facts only. Opinions, guesses, or impressions are valueless. If you are to make use of observations, reports, and data, they must be complete and correct. With this general description of the control process as a background, a more complete analysis of the term should be helpful. Actually it is used by management people, and others, in two different ways.

Control as authority

Everyone has heard, and probably used, such expressions as "Mr. Smith has control of the sales division," or "Who is in control of the laboratory?" What is really referred to is the location of the authority to initiate action. The implication is that control of an enterprise necessitates the use of authority. Only by inference, do you get the idea of control in the sense of securing adequate information about operations.

This commonplace relation between authority and control need not be confusing. The right to make management decisions includes the power to initiate and direct action as well as checking on accomplishments. It is easy to see how those in authority have a right to control what is done. Therefore, it can be assumed that control is merely the exercise of authority. However, when management is most effective, there is seldom any overt display of authority in the control of the enterprise.

The previous discussions touched on this relationship at several points. In Chapter 7, the subject of authority was presented from the conventional point of view. There it was assumed that authority is delegated from above. The reasoning is that, in theory, the head of an organization has full authority to manage its activities. He releases some of this authority by delegating it to his subordinates to relieve himself of part of his administrative burden. The need to do so was illustrated in Chapter 5 with the example of the shoe business showing how an enterprise becomes more complex as it grows.

Now that some of the other aspects of management have been considered the concept of authority should be reexamined from a slightly different angle. There are many students of management who believe authority is not delegated downward from a central source. They argue that the right to direct and control really resides in the job itself. The plant superintendent never exercises any personal authority over the maintenance shops or the motor pool. When he selects and appoints men to head these activities, their right to use authority is clearly understood as an inherent part of the assignment. They have to be able to manage in the full sense of the word.

From this point of view, by virtue of your position, you have the authority to control your operation. It is part of your job. You need not wait for someone to put it in writing. If you fail to keep fully informed of what is going on or fail to take adequate preventive and corrective actions to maintain control, you will be laying yourself open to censure.

Control as evaluation of results

More and more executives are using the word "control" in a more limited or technical sense. When they refer to the management process of controlling, they mean the various methods and devices by which they keep informed about what their subordinates are doing and whether the work is being accomplished as planned. This becomes a matter of checking up on activities, evaluating progress, and appraising the results. It requires the use of the kind of evaluative thinking described in Chapter 1.

It has been emphasized that a plan of action seldom works out exactly as anticipated. Unexpected circumstances almost always occur to affect the processing of work, the time needed to perform it, and the quantity or quality of the product. You depend on Miss Jones to get out the quarterly report, but on the day before it is due, she develops a temperature of 104 degrees and has to be sent home with the job half done. You agree to fabricate a thousand 150-pound gizmos in the next sixty days, and, in the middle of the operation, you discover someone misinterpreted the specifications on the tubes and none of them are usable. Such things can, and do, happen. They are not imagined; they are facts. You must know about them immediately if you are to meet your production goals.

Your control system must be designed to bring to your attention every fact that has any bearing on accomplishing the results you want. You must know, without any guesswork, that the work will turn out as required. You are in control of the operation only when you know it is progressing according to plan and the finished product will meet the requirements you set.

PURPOSES OF CONTROL

With this understanding of what is meant by the control process, its purposes become more clear. In management terms, they can be stated as:

1. Supplying management officials with complete, accurate, and timely information about what is being accomplished

2. Enabling them to predict any obstacles to full productivity more accurately and to take steps to eliminate or reduce the impact of such hindrances

3. As these two objectives are attained, they lead to the final goal of ensuring maximum productivity and the satisfactory accomplishment of the desired results.

Securing the information

If effective control depends upon accurate, timely information, managers must have means to secure it. Generally, you can consider that the flow of facts takes place through two main channels.

Reporting systems. All reporting is primarily for control purposes. The information that must be accumulated in a large organization is so varied that its collection becomes an extremely complicated matter, to such a degree that there is sometimes the problem of how to control the flow of control data. In your desire to be fully informed, you tend to require ever more and more reporting.

A number of different kinds of reports were mentioned in the preceding discussion. All are designed to enable responsible managers to control the activities under their direction. This purpose is not always recognized, and reporting becomes mechanical, careless, and inaccurate. Realization of the purposes for reporting tends to make the information far more accurate, intelligible, and useful for those who receive and interpret it.

Most reports reflect final accomplishments. They tell what has been done, how much, when, and by whom. Data on what is happening to the work in process or *progress reports* are equally valuable. They also show accomplishment but only partial completion. In many situations, information of this kind, in terms of major production stages, is essential to effective control.

Inspections. Reference has been made in a general way to the use of inspection techniques. This means the actual "looking into" the work product to see that it meets the requirements or specifications. Two other points must be made in this connection.

First, to judge either the quantity or the quality of the work, you must have a standard for comparison. Both the workman and the inspector must know what the standard is. The former must strive to meet the standard as he knows it, and the latter must see that the product actually does meet the standard. Again, it is apparent that if all work were perfectly performed there would be no need for quality inspections. Under normal conditions, however, supervisors must check up on the performance of their workmen. It is their responsibility not only to observe critically what is being turned out but also to make certain that the employees fully understand both the quantity and the quality requirements for satisfactory performance.

Secondly, to discharge this responsibility fully, a supervisor must take one more step. He must rigorously reject any products that do not meet the standard. Otherwise, he is condoning unsatisfactory work, nullifying the standards, and failing to meet his work goals. Rejecting unsatisfactory work means doing the job over, possibly wasting material, and adding to the cost of operation; but this is only temporary, and, in the long run, greater efficiency is achieved.

If controls are enforced, inspections are made with great frequency by the workman himself as he handles the product, and always, from time to time, by his supervisor. In addition, most large manufacturing- or assembly-type operations use specially designated inspectors to check on the acceptability of the items produced. It is not unusual for a high-level executive to check production occasionally by a personal inspection.

Another type of inspection is by surveys, usually made by a team of persons. A home office may send such a crew into a field office to review the efficiency of the work being done there. Similarly, the personnel office may schedule surveys of various aspects of personnel management. Manpower utilization surveys may be conducted to find out how well the human resources are being used. To an increasing degree, management consultant firms are being contracted to survey the segments of large organizations to find out how well the work is being managed.

All of these activities result in reports with significant information for control purposes. While they are being conducted, there may be some interference with normal work processes, but this is usually far outweighed by the improvements that result. Capable executives welcome the chance to obtain an outside evaluation of their work as a basis on which to institute even more effective management practices.

Reducing the risk

It has been stressed several times that when you assume management responsibility you automatically take on a certain amount of risk that something may occur to prevent your discharging it. It is a perfectly normal situation that all executives recognize. On the other hand, you would have more peace of mind if you can keep such risks to the minimum.

Judicious planning of your work controls can do just that; it minimizes the risks of future troubles with production. In the discussion of forecasting as part of planning in Chapter 2, it was pointed out that you have to take calculated risks but the more accurately you can predict the future, the less risk you assume. Not only is the factor of uncertainty reduced, but also, by going one step further and visualizing the possible consequences of what you propose to do, you may decide to change the sequence or nature of the action to good advantage. This ties in closely with the second purpose of controls, the prevention of future difficulties. It also illustrates once more the close relationship and interdependence between all of the management processes. In practice, forecasting and controlling are not separate entities; they are used together in varying degrees as the situation demands.

But, this is not all. Competent managers are not content just to let things happen. Their plans go far beyond merely visualizing future events and preparing to adjust to them. Good executives take the additional step of trying to shape the future as they want it. There is a great difference between simply recognizing the unfavorable events that might occur and taking steps to bring about a favorable situation.

Sometimes it is possible to prevent the circumstance from occurring. More often you must accept the possibility of it happening and use the opportunity to initiate other actions to modify its effects. If a key employee is going to retire next year, you can take the logical steps to have a fully qualified replacement ready. The troubles caused by a machine-tool breakdown can be prevented or minimized by more effective maintenance or by having a replacement unit available. During a national emergency, the labor market becomes tight at

a time when you need to expand the work force. You
give attention to new sources of recruitment, cross-tra
present employees, or engineering of jobs to utilize sem
or unskilled workers. Actions such as these do not pr ue
the happening of the future event, but they enable you to
maintain full control of the productive processes.

OBJECTS OF CONTROL

The discussion thus far has been general, referring to control of operations or work. A more complete understanding of
the process requires more specific discussion about the objects
that are controlled. In the management sense, you control
manpower, money, and materials.

Manpower controls

One of the primary goals of good management is to have
enough people with the proper qualifications to get the work
accomplished. It is equally important not to employ more
people than necessary. The larger the organization, the more
difficult it is to ensure that you have the right number of employees. Unless steps are taken to control manpower, salary
and wage costs can easily get out of hand.

Ordinarily much of this responsibility is placed on the personnel manager and his staff. They, in turn, are guided by the
requirements of operating officials and any applicable provisions of labor contracts. They decide whether requisitions
for additional employees are fully justified, the jobs are properly graded, and the existing work force is being utilized efficiently. They use their specialized knowledge to select satisfactory employees, to assist them in adjusting to their jobs,
and to motivate them to do their assigned work well. The per-

sonnel office keeps accurate records, checks on all actions that affect manpower, and reports to the front office when called upon. Another important contribution of the personnel office is in assisting operating personnel to instruct employees to do the work efficiently. Sound job training gets the workload accomplished with the minimum number of workers. Because they are staff people, personnel technicians can only recommend and advise managers in these matters. The basic responsibility for maintenance of a balanced work force rests with line managers; it is part of their managerial obligation.

In addition to the manpower controls exercised on the job or in the personnel office, the central office of a large company may also exert influence. Over-all strength limitations are often established by headquarters offices based on past experience, urgency of the task, or funds available for salaries. Ceilings are sometimes set to control the number of employees. When all the authorized positions are filled, hiring must stop except for replacements. Lower management levels are assisted in maintaining effective manpower control with such devices.

Financial controls

In a general way, everyone is aware that business enterprises have to operate within the funds available to them. This starts with the budgeting system where each year you are required to estimate your costs of operation far in advance. This in itself is an excellent control device because you must review the facts concerning future operations and justify their necessity. Briefly stated, your requests for funds are reviewed and combined with those from other parts of the company. Then, the final product is given careful study and modified as necessary by top level executives responsible for financial policy. The board of directors may have the final decision if major financing is involved.[1]

For most managers, real financial control starts when funds are made available for spending. You should keep in mind that funds are allocated to the various components of the organization on the basis of their needs, as judged by those who determine fiscal policy. A unit seldom receives all that it has asked for because the financial resources are limited and have to be spread over the entire company. What you receive, then, represents the best judgment as to what you really need. This sets your standard for spending.

Actual control at the point of spending is exercised through accounting and auditing procedures. Accurate records are kept of any amounts obligated so the budget is not exceeded. Regulations on procurement also guide using funds judiciously. After funds have been used, a further control is exercised in a review of the propriety of spending, usually made by an accountant or auditor. These people are highly trained technicians, but it is to your advantage to learn how they operate

---

[1] The Federal government operates under an unwieldy budgetary system that is often confusing to businessmen. In dealing with government agencies, it is helpful to understand some of the problems they have in maintaining financial control. Estimates of need are made in the field offices and stations of the various departments more than two years before the money is to be spent. The accumulated totals are carefully reviewed, and adjusted, at local levels, department headquarters, and the Bureau of the Budget, before they are submitted to the Appropriation Committee of the House of Representatives. At each point, justifications of the items are required, and changes may be made. This takes months. Finally, however, the recommended amounts are summarized in appropriation bills that have to be reviewed and approved by Congress before any funds become available.

Each year, agency representatives are questioned in Congressional hearings about the necessity for various budget items. Obviously, there must be a vast amount of detailed information immediately available if these questions are to be answered satisfactorily. When the hearings are over, the request goes before Congress as part of the annual appropriation bill for the agency. Passage of the act determines how much money will be available for the ensuing year.

and for what purposes so your financial dealings will be kept in order.

Another important aspect of financial control has to do with costs of operation. This is a fundamental requirement in business and industry. In the first place, you are spending funds belonging to the company and thus have a strong, ethical responsibility for their conservation. Secondly, you should try to keep costs to the minimum so your particular segment will be both stable and profitable. Through the cost-accounting system, you report what you spent or obligated and for what purposes. As indicated before, top executives need these facts to be informed about how funds are used and also to analyze them for additional economies. Thus, control data become a source of ideas for further management improvement.

In addition to the responsibility for cost reporting, everyone has a continuing obligation to analyze his own operation to secure further economies. You cannot tolerate wastes and losses due to carelessness, ignorance, or uneconomical work methods. In maintaining financial control, the degree of efficiency you achieve depends largely on your success in training and motivating your subordinates. In this effort, the example you set for them will be an important influence.

Production controls

Production controls are primarily concerned with maintaining the work processes of the unit at a relatively high level of efficiency. They focus attention on materials in process, tangible or intangible products, and methods used in production. Work reports, work measurement studies, and work improvement techniques are used to get the desired information. Frequently staff services are needed to conduct the research for such accumulations of data. Record systems and correct interpretation of records are necessary. By studying these facts, those engaged in production control can locate causes of inefficiency, waste, or other losses so they can be corrected and prevented from recurring.

Brief reference has been made to inspection procedures that check up on the quality of work at specific points in the workflow or the quality control measures. New techniques are constantly being devised. The more quickly an error in work is discovered, the less time there is wasted on further processing of an unsatisfactory item. Also, the cause of the faulty work can be eliminated so no more parts, cases, reports, or services are done wrong. Increasing attention is being given to quality control of mass-produced items through scientific sampling and inspection techniques or statistical quality control.

When a tangible product is turned out, it is relatively easy to keep track of the quantity of output. Control is maintained by review of production, progress reports, and records to find out if and where action is needed. Any drop in productivity is a signal for immediate action to find out the cause and remove it.

In other situations, exact measurement of work accomplished is difficult. If the assignment involves intangible products such as services, judgments (decisions), development of new ideas, or creation of different attitudes, the exact quantitative measures of accomplishment may be of less value than the effort to secure the measurements. In such areas there are few standards. How long should it take a lawyer to prepare a brief or try a case? How many souls should a chaplain save each month? How many decisions should an executive make daily? In such circumstances, demonstrated diligence and high quality of results may be far more significant than quantitative data.

APPLICATION OF CONTROL METHODS

As any enterprise grows, more and more decentralization takes place. From the central office down through each succeeding echelon, there are heavy retained responsibilities, but operating responsibility finally comes to rest with the work force. How are each of these higher echelons assured that it is really maintaining adequate control over the subordinate segments assigned to it? Some widely used methods and devices are described below.

Programming

Brief comments were made in Chapter 4 about programs as an important outcome of planning. Particularly in large organizations, programming is coming to be considered a significant continuing process by itself. In this sense, the word is used broadly to cover much of the three phases of the management cycle. In other words, it uses information gathered by the control system and follows through on its decisions into the action phase. Further analysis will bring out the close connection to the control process.

Program development. For example, program development, as shown earlier, is essentially a planning process. Because sound planning is always based on complete, correct information, it is natural to have close collaboration between the persons who plan the programs and those who receive, analyze, and interpret the control data. Many times, the same people perform both functions, but, if they are separated in different segments of the organization, continuous integration of the two activities is necessary.

Program execution. Once the program goes into effect,

there must be continuous checkup, appraisal of progress, and evaluation of results. Inspections and production reports are routine. Standards are applied vigorously. This is the control process in action, but it is taking place concurrently with the executive action phase of the management cycle. It was stated as a basic principle that planning takes place continuously throughout the entire area of management. Now it becomes apparent that control actions also are going on continuously.

Review and analysis. The final stage of programming is usually called "review and analysis." At this point, the reports from operating units are studied at each level to determine how well the program is succeeding and to find out how results can be improved. Clearly, this is what was defined as the control process. But action does not stop with study of the data. More decisions are made as replanning takes place, and the management cycle is in full swing again. Chapter 10 discusses the review and analysis techniques more fully.

Interpretation of findings

The review and analysis stage of programming is aimed almost entirely at interpretation of information received through the control system. What takes place when you interpret these facts merits further consideration.

There is little reason for any record-keeping system unless it pays its way. A reporting system that fails to present essential facts or give all the details necessary for a true picture is worse than useless. It may lead management astray instead of guiding it to its goal. But, adequate data alone are not enough. Each set of facts must be interpreted and its meaning determined in relation to reports from other units. This calls for the highest type of ability to analyze and make sound deductions. If reports indicate Section A is falling behind in production, the effect on other areas must be taken into consideration in addition to the possible steps to eliminate troubles in Section A. Interpretation of facts often leads to a problem-solving situation where a decision must be made and action taken.

The management man who seeks to keep firm control seizes every opportunity to develop his ability to interpret information. Many techniques can be used, from the scientific procedures of the trained statistician to the grass-root device of asking oneself a series of questions about the facts under consideration. Three commonly used methods will be discussed briefly.

Comparison. An isolated figure or fact often has little meaning, but, when it is compared with similar information, a meaningful relationship usually appears. If you are told that the storage division handled 982 ton-miles of materials last week, you have a fact but that is all. If further study discloses that the figure for the previous week was only 800 ton-miles, that the average for last year was only 860, or that the same work force in Plant B handles an average of 1150 ton-miles per week, you begin to see the significance. You have made meaningful comparisons.

Seeking the deviant. It has been said that many success-ful executives pay little attention to what is progressing suc-cessfully but start immediate action if they find something going wrong. When you interpret facts, you are not always looking for what is wrong. You are also seeking any indication of a deviation from the normal. A change may or may not be significant, but it is worth trying to find out what is causing it. Deviants in an unfavorable direction, such as rising costs, decreased production, and heavier employee turnover, usually stimulate prompt action. However, similar inquiry about the causes of increased efficiency may also be valuable. You often make discoveries that can be passed on to others with equally good results.

Charting. The visual presentation of data is used so commonly today that charts have become the symbol of an executive. They have innumerable uses and applications. The most useful charts are simple and portray the situation clearly. Probably bar graphs like the two that follow are most com-

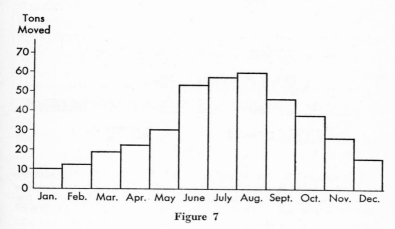

Figure 7

monly used, but line charts, pie charts, flow charts, and many other types are also common.

Production figures, employment turnover, waste, errors, or progress can all be put in visual form for instant interpretation. The huge thermometers used to show progress in charity drives or similar campaigns illustrate a simple form of charting that can be applied to many work situations. Figure 7 indicates how clearly one can compare the tons moved by a labor unit during various months of the year.

A more complicated control chart, known as the Gantt chart, is described in most books on industrial management because it is widely used in industry. Its primary purpose is usually to assist production control by recording progress against predicted goals. It is subject to wide variation and can be adapted for use in an office as well as in a factory. Many elaborate modifications in the form of control boards to be placed on the wall have been patented for sale. Below is a simple illustration of one (Figure 8).

GANTT MAN RECORD CHART

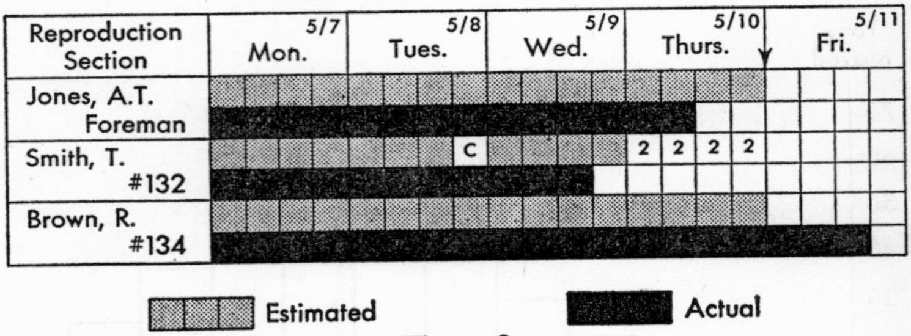

Reproduction Section	5/7 Mon.			5/8 Tues.			5/9 Wed.			5/10 Thurs.			5/11 Fri.		
Jones, A.T. Foreman															
Smith, T. #132				C						2	2	2	2		
Brown, R. #134															

▓▓▓ Estimated   ███ Actual

Figure 8

Explanation: The chart is read as of c.o.b. May 10th. The Foreman was present but failed to get estimated production completed as scheduled on Thursday night. This was largely because Smith lost 2 hours in a conference on Tuesday, and took Thursday off. Brown has worked all week and is 6 hours ahead of schedule.

CORRECTIVE ACTIONS

It has been emphasized a number of times that because the original plans do not always work out exactly as expected, it is necessary to check on the results of executive actions. This checkup is the heart of the control system. Sometimes the cause of the trouble is so obvious that the correction is equally apparent. More often you have to search behind the situation. After the cause is discovered, you have to replan your approach to secure the results you want. Prompt corrective action is necessary whenever you discover unsatisfactory situations. These changes usually involve the technical work procedures, equipment, or personnel at the work site. You cannot assume, however, that the fault is always at the operating level.

In a pamphlet entitled "Universals in Management Planning and Controlling" issued in 1954 by the American Management Association, J. M. Juran makes an interesting point. He notes that study of any existing situation or procedure must be based on its present level of effectiveness. This may be far below what you desire and much less than what is feasible. Rather than indicating a need for a new procedure, all that might be necessary may be better management of what now exists. In such a situation, *any* procedure will fail to produce maximum results and efforts spent on improving work methods are largely wasted until management deficiencies are removed. He points out that one of the choices for corrective action is to make better use of the present setup.

Regardless of the corrective measures taken, you cannot be content if the situation might recur. Because this is so frequently the case, it is a good rule always to consider the steps necessary to prevent the trouble in the future. This, of course, calls for action quite different from that taken to correct the condition. Often you are content to warn those responsible, but good management suggests taking more positive actions, if necessary, to remove the cause and prevent repetition of the difficulty.

OTHER ASPECTS OF CONTROL

Assessing blame

The emphasis above was placed on finding out what is wrong. When you do identify a trouble spot, there is a natural tendency to look for a culprit. It is valuable to know who made the mistake so you can take steps to strengthen him and avoid repetition of the error. This is good management. But, to use the circumstance to blame the unfortunate employee is not.

No one likes to be embarrassed by having his mistakes magnified. The morale of the employee is already lowered by realization of his failure. To depress it even more serves no useful purpose and may create resentment that will aggravate the condition. The control process is designed to prevent and alleviate difficulties rather than increase them. The wise manager, in his discussions with employees responsible for unsatisfactory conditions, concentrates on arousing the desire to bring about the necessary improvement. If discipline is required, it should be based upon a thorough study of the employee. Control measures involve the work for which the employee is responsible.

Supervision as control

As a supervisor, you are aware of the varied nature of your own responsibilities. One of these is to be fully informed about what is happening in your unit. Much of your information comes from personal observation as you go about your duties. What you see and learn by talking with subordinates is important but does not give the full story.

You need a continuing flow of significant data so you can review it, analyze it, compare it, and discover how well you are doing. Within your own organizational unit, you can plan a simple but sufficient control system to tell you if you are getting out the work as required. With such a system you are also in a position to supply higher echelons the information they need.

Controllership

The maintenance of adequate controls, like other management processes, can become complicated. Recognizing this, many businesses have established positions for controllers on various levels to provide specialized assistance to operating managers. Controllership is built around the central function of providing significant information to those who manage. In discharging his responsibility, the controller places a great deal of importance on a sound plan of financial management. He often employs specialists to handle budget matters, cost accounting, program review and analysis, or work improvements. If they are available, these technicians can give valuable help in achieving control of your operations.

Overcontrol

In large organizations, there is always a problem of how to maintain the flow of necessary information for control purposes. Each headquarters and each staff office may set forth its own requirements and institute its own reporting system. The result may be a heavy duplication of report data, unnecessary work preparing the reports, and even a lack of agreement between the facts submitted. Furthermore, there is a tendency to ask for information that is seldom or never used, or already available from other sources.

In similar vein, higher levels in the organization may set unnecessarily high standards or impose unrealistic fund and strength limitations. Such standards reduce rather than increase operating efficiency. Badly conceived control measures are as much as indication of poor management as confused organizational structures or lack of intelligible directions.

To avoid such situations, it is frequently necessary to employ report-control officers. Their major duty is to study each request for additional information to establish its validity. They also try to coordinate the reporting system by combining forms and eliminating any that are not justified. In this way, they keep the control process from getting out of hand.

Electronic devices

One further aspect of the control process should be noted. This is the recent development and utilization of automatic control devices. They are applied in two directions.

One is the so-called electronic brains into which vast amounts of factual data are fed and out of which answers are obtained in minutes that would otherwise take the combined efforts of many specialists for a long time. These scientific wonders are being used more and more for control data and other purposes. Automatic data processing systems are being installed in business establishments as fast as the the machines can be built and people trained to use them.

The second method is the application of electronic controls directly to machine tools so they become almost completely self-controlled. As time goes on, this form of automation will probably be used to an increasing degree in production plants. The average shop superintendent should explore the possibility of increasing efficiency through these devices even though he will have to depend upon the technical know-how of highly specialized engineers and scientists to make the actual decisions. There are tremendous opportunities for economies in this area. Production engineers are talking of the automatic factory as a near possibility. The use of these devices in appropriate operations is certain to increase rapidly.

SUMMARY

Controlling the work was the last phase of the management cycle and of the five management processes to be studied. Without control, a business would be subject to unknown influences that would eventually destroy it. Only disaster can result from lack of control.

In this chapter, it was stressed that although some people use the word "control" to refer to authority or power, its correct usage in the management sense is in connection with securing the information necessary to ensure efficient operations and achieve the purposes of the enterprise. The methods and devices described have been used to correct conditions that result in inefficiency and to take steps to prevent similar conditions in the future.

Finally, as you check on the progress and results of your work, you frequently uncover situations that call for replanning. Thus, what you tentatively thought was the end of the management cycle actually triggers the start of a new round by setting up new goals and supplying information for more planning. The competent manager is constantly applying the management processes to his personnel, his finances, and his work procedures. Control systems are in continuous action in modern business enterprises along with planning and executive action.

PART FIVE

Applying the Management Processes

The preceding chapters have described the five basic management processes and shown how they interact in the management cycle. With this background, it is possible to explore some of the ways in which these processes are applied to work operations and to estimate to some degree how they can be applied in the future.

10

Techniques of Management

Many practical methods of applying the management processes to work situations have already been given. Most of them
can be considered the more simple managerial techniques
that are easily learned and commonly used by successful
executives. There are others, however, that are more complicated and for this reason usually used only by trained
specialists. Brief descriptions of some of these more technical
methods are presented in this chapter.

RELATION OF SKILL TO UNDERSTANDING

Management has been defined as doing certain things:
planning, making decisions, organizing, directing, coordinating,
and controlling. These are acts and to perform them well takes
a high degree of skill. Practice in performance until efficiency
is achieved is necessary to become skillful. Therefore, you
must practice the techniques of good management to become
a good manager.

As stated in the preface, the fundamental purpose of this
book is not to develop managerial skills but to lay a foundation of understanding so the actions are more meaningful

and purposeful. Anyone attempting to develop competence in a new field is usually helped by securing a basic knowledge of the subject from others. This approach assumes that skill in performing the specific acts involved is developed more rapidly and more soundly in the long run if there is an understanding of the nature and purpose of the acts first. For the most part, training in the techniques will follow by individual efforts to use better managerial methods on the job, assistance and coaching from others, or formal training in ways to manage more effectively.

Achieving goals

Throughout the book, it has been mentioned frequently that all efforts of management must be purposeful. Setting goals was considered a prerequisite to effective planning; every component part of an organization must have clearly defined objectives. Every act of the responsible executive and his subordinates must contribute directly or indirectly to attaining the objectives.

The job of the manager, then, is to plan the operations under his direction so the established goals will be achieved efficiently. To do this, he must clearly understand the objectives, ensure a similar degree of understanding by his employees, and effectively utilize all the available resources at his command.

The human element

No marvel of science has been invented yet to replace the human brain. Management is still a responsibility of people. Because everyone differs in background, interests, attitudes, and abilities, each will manage differently. No two persons would use their job resources in exactly the same way, yet each might achieve excellent results.

One of the basic characteristics of a good executive is his ability to get work performed by others. Here again, the human element comes to the fore. Not only do you have to become proficient in the management of your financial and material resources and the procedures involved, but you also have to achieve a high degree of understanding of, and skill in, the techniques of personnel management.

THE TOOLS OF MANAGEMENT

There are many ways, methods, procedures, and techniques by which you can attain your management goals successfully. The preceding chapters described many ways to handle work effectively. You are already using some of them to good advantage. Others you can learn to use skillfully without too great an effort. However, some are so technical and complex that you may never find the time or opportunity to develop full skill in their use. If you are to be a competent executive, you will probably not find it possible to become a time and motion expert, job classifier, or organization and methods analyst as well.

You can think of the tools of management, therefore, as falling into two categories. The first covers the practical and useful techniques used from day to day in the management of your operations. The second group includes the more complicated methods and devices that require long training and experience for expert use. These are the techniques supplied by staff specialists. Even though you may not be able to use them yourself, you should know about them so you can make use of them to improve the management of your operations.

Because new and improved techniques are constantly being

discovered, all that can be done here is to point out the general nature of such methods. By knowing the areas in which special techniques have been perfected, you will be able to request the staff assistance you need to solve your own management problems. You will also be able to cooperate more fully with these technicians if their work brings them into your part of the organization. In consonance with the management philosophy followed throughout, these methods will be discussed under the three basic phases of the management cycle: planning, executive action, and control.

PLANNING TECHNIQUES

The discussion of the planning process in Chapters 3 and 4 included many suggestions on how to plan your work. As was noted, you will be using some of these ideas in your day-to-day operations. Some additional methods of carrying on the planning process follow. You should be familiar with them even though they may not apply to your present job.

Production planning

Wherever a product is involved, managers must give careful attention to the creation of that product. Manufacturing is, of course, a typical example. Such conditions normally occur in shops of many types and to a limited degree in some research and development activities. However, the product does not always have to be a tangible one. It is both possible and highly desirable to plan for the production of services, the disposition of cases, the handling of stores, or the development of written materials.

The purpose of planning, of course, is to make certain the

required productivity is accomplished as efficiently as possible. It must be assumed that the planner has adequate information about what is to be produced, how much, and how soon. This includes any necessary specifications on quality, finish, capacity, or similar matters. These actually set up a requirement to meet. When you know exactly what this requirement is, you can plan how to meet it. Three major work aspects are involved:

1. The materials on which the work is to be performed or supplies of any kind
2. The equipment needed for the processing, such as tools, jigs, machines, furniture, or accessories required in the procedures
3. The manpower to turn out the product or direct labor required

These represent the three physical items in the list of basic management elements: materials, machines, and men. Production planning sees that these essentials are available in the proper quantity when needed. Because you are aiming at efficient work, you plan their use in connection with the two remaining elements: money and methods.

Simply stated, the production engineer plans in advance how the product materials are to be handled so they will be on hand when needed, in sufficient quantity and adequate quality and at the lowest feasible cost. In developing such plans, he may call upon appropriate line and staff employees for the information he needs. When his plans are complete and approved by the appropriate executive, they go to the line-operating people to be carried out.

Here again, clear and complete communication is necessary. If you, as a manager, fail to understand exactly what is expected of you, you will fail in your part of the production plan. In large organizations with diverse and complicated activities, the failure of one assignment can delay or completely upset a major operation. Therefore, it is extremely important for you to understand your part in any production plan so each dollar expended will secure the greatest possible return in production value.

Review and analysis

Planning leads to executive actions that in turn must be appraised to see whether the objectives are being attained efficiently. If your control system reveals inadequacies, further planning is required to determine what new actions are necessary. Because most operations are of a continuing nature, replanning is constantly occurring. The data from the reporting system, inspections, and surveys must be carefully evaluated to find out their significance. This is the review and analysis technique mentioned briefly in Chapter 9. Here is how it works.

The facts and figures on progress and accomplishment are brought together at the lowest levels. Here they are studied to see whether or not they reveal any hints on how operations can be improved. If they do, replanning and corrective measures can take place immediately. The main responsibility at this point, however, is to secure accurate facts to be sent up to the next level.

Here, information from several subordinate segments flows together and data from different sources are compared. Skilled analysts review the facts and apply appropriate analytical techniques to draw all possible meaning out of the data available. Again, ideas for improvement are translated into action. At each level steps may be taken

To redirect present operations
To evaluate the soundness of past accomplishments
To develop future plans and programs

The final results show particularly in the development of long-range estimates, major action programs, and the budget. All of these are planning activities.

This review and analysis makes use of the control techniques discussed in Chapter 9. To a degree, all alert executives use these methods to improve the efficiency of their operations. The trained analyst, however, has more tools available, such as the modern statistical techniques, by which additional meaning can be obtained from raw data.

Budget formulation

Chapter 9 also pointed out that one of the basic aspects of financial management is the preparation of the budget. Although occasional references are made to manpower budgets, time budgets, or even supply budgets, the term is restricted here to the annual estimate or forecast of money requirements to operate the business. Like any planning, there must be adequate and accurate facts upon which to base the budget. Whether the business is large or small, the source of these facts is found at the lowest level of operation where the work is actually performed. After a decision is made about the nature of operations for the next year, realistic estimates can be made on how much it will cost to carry on the portion of the work assigned to each organizational unit.

These estimates are collected and studied with great care. Foremen and managers may be asked for additional justifications for their requests. Their planning should take into consideration the manpower necessary, the supplies and materials required, the machines and tools needed, and the methods to be used.

At higher levels, it may become evident that estimates at lower levels should be modified because of the needs of other segments, possible changes in the national or international scene, financial limitations, or other valid reasons.

When the budget is finally completed, it constitutes the financial plan for the ensuing year. Each part of the enterprise is told exactly how much of the total fiscal resources it is to have and each is expected to operate accordingly.

The planning conference

Conferences are a fairly common way to plan work. By getting together the key individuals concerned with the matter under discussion, all of the significant points of view can be expressed and coordinated. Such a group brings together the meaningful facts on which sound decisions can be based. By participating in the planning process, the individuals become well informed on what is contemplated and also feel greater responsibility for carrying out the plan agreed upon.

But, unless they are well planned, such meetings can be wasteful. The time of a group of executives and technicians represents a heavy cost. Too often the results obtained are not commensurate with the time expended. On the other hand, carefully planned and skillfully conducted conferences achieve superior results. Training in conference leadership can contribute to the development of such competence. Many businesses conduct courses for this purpose or arrange for their executives to attend outside training sessions.

TECHNIQUES FOR EXECUTIVE ACTION

As emphasized previously, plans are meaningless unless they are carried out. Yet, securing effective action is often a serious problem. First, full communication must be established with every person involved in the implementation. Secondly, everyone must be motivated to do his part willingly and efficiently. Often both of these needs are largely met by the planning conferences discussed above. More specific ways to secure executive action were presented in Chapters 5 through 8. Other techniques you should know about follow.

Programming

The planning discussed above culminates in certain decisions or actions to be taken. This represents the first step in programming, program development. The second is usually called program execution and is the phase to be discussed here. The third and last stage is program review and analysis which is the method of replanning that grows out of the control process (see p. 173).

A program has been defined as a fairly stable plan of action that continues over a considerable period of time (see Chapter 4). It might also be described as a scheme of administrative action designed to accomplish a definite objective. Both are correct from slightly different points of view. Note, however, in the second statement the phrase "a scheme of administrative action." This is the aspect under consideration.

Ideally, a program statement furnishes such clear directions that all who read it see exactly what their parts are; they know what to do and how to do it. In this sense programming automatically results in a pattern of executive action. Each level in the organization develops its own program to meet its own objectives. Each emerges with its own scheme of action.

It is important to remember that many different programs are necessary and must be operated concurrently. In addition to broad sales and manufacturing programs and subsidiary advertising and production plans, there are more specific schemes of administrative action, such as an employee retirement program or a three-year construction program. Each one contributes to the broad objectives, and each describes the type of executive action required.

Many projects will also be completed within the program areas. Just as with programming, a project must tell clearly what actions are necessary to bring it to a conclusion. Each one is an assignment of a certain amount of work to be accomplished, such as the building of a warehouse or the development of a new product. The project defines the kind of action to be taken.

Increasing use is being made of specialists to secure effective programming. New techniques such as linear and mathematical programming require especially trained persons. This is a rapidly expanding field often related to the use of electronic devices for problem solving and automatic data processing.

Work orders

In manufacturing operations, it is common to use work orders. Although primarily a control device, these orders are also extremely useful in showing what kind of work is required and where it is to be performed. Because they specify and schedule the flow of the work, they help to secure the appropriate executive action.

Organization charts

One result of planning is the establishment of the organizational structure. This action has far-reaching results that were described in Chapters 5 and 6. Although you have a share in any action to change your own organizational pattern, the staff specialists in this function, often known as organization and methods analysts, also have an important part.

The charts portraying organizational relationships may play a significant role in determining executive action. A direct effect is in indicating who does what. In other words, the chart both separates the different kinds of operations and at the same time binds them together into an integrated and coordinated whole. A further effect is in the pattern of delegation. The relations between segments as depicted by the chart indicate how responsibility for action is passed down from one level to another.

Operations research

The latest and by far the most technical tool or technique to help management find solutions to fundamental management problems is operations research. The word "operations" here means a broad aspect of what is happening in the enterprise. In other words, the research is applied to problems affecting an organization as a whole; it is not applicable to the minor routine operating problems. Operations research has been defined as the application of the scientific method to the study of management problems. It seeks practical answers by providing executives with a quantitative basis for decision. It does not supply the answer directly; it merely supplements the judgment of the executive.

Briefly stated, this method uses any applicable scientific technique with major reliance on statistical theory and higher mathematics. These include such concepts as the theory of probability, linear programming, symbolic logic, the theory of decision, the theory of games, and the search theory. Because of the diverse nature of these tools and the additional requirement of competence in engineering, mathematics, and human relations, a team of analysts is often required. It should be noted, however, that in many situations valuable results can be obtained with the use of arithmetic. The complexity of the problem determines the type of techniques to be used.

Not all management problems can be resolved with operations research. In the first place, only situations that are definable in quantitative terms can be attacked with this method. Secondly, the complete data on all aspects of the problem must be available for the analysts. A further difficulty lies in communication between the operating officials and the analysts. This is often critical in the interpretation of the recommendations by the executives concerned.

There are two controlling characteristics. The first is the inclusive nature of the studies. All pertinent aspects of the problem are covered as a basis for broad policy decisions and any known science and its methodology can be used to arrive at practical conclusions. Secondly, the research must be related to the top level of the managerial structure. The team must be in continuous, close contact with the administrative head and his immediate subordinates. This improves communication, ensures mutual understanding at the policy-making level, and facilitates access to any desired information.

This technique has been used in both business and industry

for many purposes. Some of the areas where major improvements have been reported are in petroleum, railroad, aircraft, automobile, steel, and chemical industries. They cover such problem areas as inventory, production, parts, time standards, budgeting, sales, and many others. Extensive use of the method in military affairs has also produced some amazing results. One study made during World War II is reported to have increased the effectiveness of depth bombs used by the British Navy by 500 per cent.

Business usually tries to measure the results of effects in dollar savings. There are, however, many other possible and probable benefits, such as increased awareness of problems, better definition of objectives, improved practices, stimulation of ideas, and better acceptance of changes. Even negative results can be helpful to avoid erroneous decisions and identify poor methods. Other effects that may be secured are:

1. More objectivity is introduced
2. Guesses and shallow answers are reduced
3. Goals are clarified
4. Better yardsticks are made available
5. New methods for problem-solving evolve

Finally, it should be stated that operations research is not designed to replace the executive. His mature judgment based on experience must be brought to bear on any recommendations, and he still must assume the responsibility for making the management decisions.

In the McKinsey Foundation lectures given before the Graduate School of Business at Columbia University, Ralph J. Cordiner pointed out that the greatest value of such processes may be in helping managers to see the business as a whole, to plan with greater confidence, and to communicate the plans more clearly to others.

CONTROL TECHNIQUES

To maintain control, management officials must have a continuous flow of timely, accurate, and meaningful information. Sources and methods of securing these data were discussed in Chapter 9 with emphasis on reporting. Everyone recognizes how onerous, time-consuming, and expensive a reporting system can become. There is always a tendency to ask for more information than is actually needed. Different offices may ask for the same data. A report to meet a temporary need may continue long after the need is gone. Some executives have difficulty distinguishing between what is necessary and what is merely desirable. For these reasons, all large organizations give continuing attention to the problem of planning and controlling the control system itself.

It was pointed out earlier that at the lower levels of management, the primary responsibility is to see that the proper facts are collected and forwarded. Even though the system dictates what information is wanted, you have to use judgment in selecting the data and care to ensure its accuracy. You have a further responsibility to analyze these facts to see if you can improve your own operation.

At higher levels, there are several problems. The first is getting all the reports in on time so the full picture can be seen before it is too late to be significant. Then, there is the necessity of summarizing the data, getting the right figures together, and avoiding adding "peaches" to "apples." Finally, to utilize the facts, they must be analyzed to determine the trends, the deviants, and the actions to be taken. A few of the specialized techniques used by management officials to maintain control follow. To some extent these overlap the methods discussed in Chapter 9.

Manpower utilization

In both World Wars, there has been an all-out effort to bring the total national strength to bear to secure a victorious result. This meant utilizing the civilian population as well as military forces to the best advantage. In these situations, strong efforts were made to recruit, train, and put at productive work many persons with limited job abilities. The successful employment of such marginal workers demonstrated the importance of planning to achieve better utilization of the work force at all times.

Because management is constantly striving for greater efficiency, it is natural that increasing attention is focused on manpower costs. Control is necessary to prevent expenditures for direct and indirect labor from getting out of hand.

One of the ways to solve this problem is through the use of hiring standards. Jobs are analyzed to determine exactly what is required to fill them satisfactorily. These standards are formulated to ensure the employment of better qualified employees. Work load studies are used to determine the numbers of employees necessary to carry on specified operations. All of these devices are guides for self-control and enable the analysts at higher levels to interpret the manpower data assembled from reports and surveys more intelligently.

Within the personnel offices of large organizations, a position control file is often maintained from two sources. The basic one is the number of positions authorized by management. The second is the flow of personnel actions that change the status of persons who fill these authorized positions. With these data, it is possible to tell at any time the authorized strength, the actual strength, and the size of the recruitment effort necessary to fill the vacancies.

Another aspect of manpower control to secure better personnel utilization is the continuing analysis of attendance data such as resignations, turnover, unauthorized absence, and sick leave. The more fully you can keep employees on the job, the better you can utilize their abilities. Certainly you cannot get anything out of them if they are absent. Replacements also represent a staggering expense. Using a nominal estimate of only $200 as the cost of replacing the average worker, a business could spend many millions a year merely to maintain its work force. It is no wonder personnel officers and line executives are cooperating to reduce turnover.

Financial control methods

Besides the various accounting techniques and budgetary devices already discussed, another effective control over expenditures is exercised through the system of fund allocation. This results from a thorough study of data showing the patterns of expenditures related to the projects assigned.

Normally, the controller or accounting office prepares a document that sets forth the various categories for which funds can be spent or obligated. It also indicates amounts available for various purposes. On this basis, funds are then allocated to the various components of the enterprise, proportionate to their needs. Often allocations are made on a quarterly basis to ensure a spread of activity throughout the year and to prevent complete exhaustion of funds in the last quarter.

Inventory control

In big business, the problem of controlling the amounts of physical items on hand becomes a tremendous task. It is necessary to have an adequate supply of materials, parts, tools, and equipment available to prevent work from being delayed or halted. On the other hand, it is easy to accumulate fantastic quantities of such things that are far beyond the real immediate needs.

Further problems in this connection take many forms. One is the tying up of literally billions of dollars in inventories. Another is the factor of obsolescence if supplies become outdated and useless. A third is depreciation which, again, renders the materials useless or reclaimable only after expensive reworking. Finally, there is the problem of locating what is required and making it available when and where it is needed.

Persons who have even limited responsibility for stocks of physical items can contribute substantially to the alleviation of some of the problems mentioned above. Good management principles should lead you to keep strict control of your inventories, to inspect them frequently, to avoid deterioration of stocks, and to reduce quantities to the lowest practicable level.

SUMMARY

The specialized management techniques discussed in this chapter represent only a few of those available. They are, however, illustrative of many more that are used by specialists and technicians. Others, such as statistical or quality control methods, have been mentioned in previous chapters. No attempt has been made to describe these techniques in detail because a general knowledge of them is sufficient unless the reader intends to become a management technician.

As the manager of your own unit, however, you need an understanding of the nature and purpose of these tools for several reasons. When specialists come into your work area to make management studies, you can be more helpful to them if you have some idea of what they are doing. Also, you can use the opportunity to learn more about the methods they use. They usually respond quickly to a person who shows an interest in and some familiarity with their methods. Finally, you are in a better position to ask for technical assistance if you know such techniques are available. All of these increase your competence as a skilled manager and the contribution you make.

11

Improving Work Methods

Increased efficiency is a principal goal of management. Therefore, it is only natural that numerous references to the improvement of work methods have been made in previous chapters. Every supervisor and executive recognizes his responsibility in this area. To became a competent manager, you should look closely at some of the tried and proved methods of improving the work of your unit.

PRINCIPLES

There must be a continual effort to effect better management. As a frame of reference for your planning, here are a few principles that might be helpful.

Work methods can be improved. The possibilities of achieving better results are inexhaustible. For example, literally thousands of improvements have been made in methods of washing clothes and more are being found all of the time. Manufacturers would like people to believe they have achieved perfection in home laundries, but even better models will be advertised in the future.

Everyone has the innate ability to devise better methods.
Creative ideas can be stimulated in everyone. The kind of
leadership that stimulates new ideas releases an endless
source of job improvements.

*Your responsibility for economy and efficiency requires
your constant attention to these opportunities.* You, and every
one who works with you, should constantly be searching for
answers to the question, "How can we do it better?"

*Because human beings tend to resist change, you must
develop their attitudes not only to accept improved methods
but also to initiate them.* This part of management requires
a spark plug, someone to fire the imagination of others.

There are two basic attitudes that must be developed if you
are to apply these principles to achieve better work methods.
The first is alertness to situations where improvements can be
made fruitfully. It is easy to walk past work operations day
after day without noticing they are inefficient. The second is
willingness to question the existing work methods. Almost
every improvement has come about because someone questioned what was being done. Even standardized operating
procedures are not sacred. They exist because at a given time
someone thought they were the best way, but they should be
changed when they are outmoded or when better methods are
found.

IMPROVING THE WORK OF A GROUP

If you are alert to situations where improvement appears
feasible and are willing to question existing methods, you
have the correct attitude to secure more efficient work procedures. But, that is not enough; you have to do something to
get the change made. First, it is necessary to consider some of

the practical ways of improving the work processes of a unit as a whole.

The informal method

The title used here merely introduces the common-sense process of standing back and sizing up the total situation. It is desirable to do this from time to time to get a view of the whole operation of the unit. In the round of daily duties, a supervisor may not get the full picture of over-all flow of work. The following points should be stressed:

Compare the actual activities going on in the unit to the true functions assigned to it. A functional organization chart or any current statement of the functions of the unit will help. The purpose is to review what is expected from the unit and compare it with what actually goes on. If extraneous activities have crept in or if some tasks are no longer necessary, the situation should be corrected as quickly as possible.

Review the general layout, methods, and equipment in relation to the purpose of the unit. An over-all view of the total operation keeps the mind open for ideas.

Question any aspects of the work of the unit that seem unsatisfactory. The key questions here are:

Is this operation necessary?
Where should it be performed?
When should it be done?
How should it be done?

Discuss with others the ideas for work improvement that emerge. Members of the work group should be able to make helpful suggestions. In nearly all cases, a supervisor wants to talk to *his* supervisor about the changes he is contemplating.

Make the adjustments. After you have assured yourself

that you actually can improve your work operations, you certainly will want to try out the improvements. Careful observation to be sure they work out satisfactorily is a requirement, and you will normally want help in the evaluation from others, such as your superior and appropriate specialists who are available.

Management surveys

A complete survey involves a thorough review and analysis of the management of every aspect of an organizational segment. It requires a team of qualified specialists who must spend considerable time exploring the purpose or objective, the organizational structure, the efficiency of methods in use, utilization of the work force, productivity, costs of operation, and many related aspects. For your purpose, you can simplify this process by considering the techniques you could use to make a survey of your own unit. Although three kinds of surveys are mentioned, they usually overlap in actual practice. In looking at your organization, you will get ideas about improving work methods and utilizing the work force and vice versa.

Organizational surveys are valuable as a starting point because they help give a fresh view of the organization as a whole. Probably you would begin with a thoughtful review of the current organization chart, the goals of the unit, and the functions being performed. It might also help at this point to review Chapters 5 and 6, particularly the part dealing with reorganizing a unit. To stimulate thinking, questions like the following can be posed:

1. Purpose of the unit
   a. What is the objective?
   b. Is it clearly understood by all employees?

     c. Are any functions of the unit duplicated elsewhere in the organization? Is it necessary?

2. Relationships

     a. How does the objective contribute to the larger goal of the installation?

     b. Does each subordinate part of the unit understand its function?

     c. Are similar types of work grouped together, or are they scattered in several places?

     d. Is there free communication up, down, and across?

     e. Is there more evidence of authority than of leadership?

     f. Is there any evidence of misunderstanding, antagonism, or failure to cooperate? Where? Why?

3. Work load

     a. Does any one segment appear to be more heavily worked than others? Why?

     b. Is there an excessive backlog of work? What caused it?

     c. Is the pace of work normal? Fast? Slow?

Methods surveys focus attention on how the work is being performed. Normally a manager approaches this problem by singling out the activity that consumes the most man-hours because any improvement here means more saving than in a minor operation. The more technical ways of making these analyses, such as the work distribution chart and the process analysis chart, will be discussed later. It is desirable, however, that in your day-to-day work you use the opportunity to question the efficiency of your work methods. As in other forms of analysis, it requires a critical attitude. Some questions you might ask are:

1. Work flow

     a. Does the work come in evenly or not?

     b. Does it pile up before you start acting on it?

  c. Are there significant delays in processing it? Where?
  Why?

  d. Does work leave the unit on time?

2. Methods

  a. In general, are methods appropriate for the nature of
  the work?

  b. Can the major steps in the process be easily identified?
  Are they all really necessary? Why?

  c. Where is the most time consumed? Why?

  d. Is equipment appropriate for the work? Is it up to
  date and efficient?

  e. Does much work have to be done over? Why?

  f. Do inspections or other control measures interfere
  with efficiency?

  g. Do any of the employees have good ideas about improving the processing of the work?

Questions like these stimulate the flow of ideas, and they
invariably lead to practical changes for greater efficiency.

Manpower utilization surveys direct attention to the work
force, which is the primary resource of job skills and knowledge necessary to get the work accomplished. Because people
are involved, you have to consider not only their abilities and capacities but also their morale, e.g., motivation or
the will to work. Some of the aspects are disclosed by use of
the work distribution chart to be described later. They also
can be attacked by the question and answer approach:

1. Attitudes

  a. Do employees appear to be happy? Listless? Fearful?
  Tense?

  b. Is there any evidence of loafing?

  c. Are complaints and grievances numerous or serious?
  Are they handled promptly?

    d. Do employees work well together as a team?

    e. Do they show initiative and resourcefulness in unusual situations?

2. Job skills and knowledge

    a. Is training of new employees performed satisfactorily and promptly?

    b. Do employees appear to be confused about what they are expected to do?

    c. Do they stop work frequently to ask questions about the job?

    d. Is any planned training in skills being conducted?

3. Assignments

    a. Are all employees engaged in useful work?

    b. Is the work load evenly balanced?

    c. How much overtime is needed?

    d. Are there problems connected with job ratings?

    e. Are workers doing what their job sheets specify?

4. Supervision

    a. Do supervisors have enough authority to discharge their responsibilities?

    b. How much time do they spend out on the floor? In their offices?

    c. Are their appraisals of employee performance sound? Are they followed by appropriate actions?

    d. Is the use of leave normal? Better than normal? Worse than normal? Why?

    e. Are employee turnover statistics satisfactory?

    f. Are reports a serious problem?

These suggestions show how you can make management surveys by using the resources right at hand, your own initiative and the help of your employees. From time to time, more technical surveys of your unit may be made by teams of specialists. These instances provide excellent opportunities for you to become more familiar with the professional methods used by the analysts and to secure the utmost improvement as a result of their surveys.

IMPROVING THE WORK OF AN INDIVIDUAL EMPLOYEE

Eventually any analyses you make of the operations and processes used by the work force as a group will lead you back to a study of how well each employee is doing his part. At this point, there is a person-to-person contact with all the hazards of normal human relations. Where you expect understanding, cooperation, and enthusiasm, you may find apathy, resentment, and even antagonism. You need to be particularly sensitive to your own feelings toward a worker and his job because your attitude has a lot to do with how he feels about work improvement.

This gives a clue to a fundamental truth about human relations: before a leader can get the willing cooperation of his followers, he must establish a mutual relationship of confidence and respect. Or, in the reverse, you cannot expect to improve the work methods of an employee until he is willing to make the desired change.

To establish such an attitude, you should try to put yourself in the place of the employee. If you were doing his work, what would make you want to improve the methods? There must be an incentive strong enough to overcome the objections to changing his work habits. Loyalty to the employer or personal friendliness for you may do the trick. More frequently it is necessary to appeal to an individual's self-interest. It will make the job easier, safer, and more pleasant. Economies effected might eventually mean higher grade levels or more opportunities for advancement. The employee's prestige will be enhanced. Recognition of the worker as an important contributor to the improvement may be all that is necessary.

The two main ways in which these problems are handled will be discussed briefly.

Time and motion study

This phrase usually refers to a technique by which accurate data are obtained on the length of time it takes to perform the various motions of a certain task. It has been used most frequently with repetitive actions involving machines, tools, and body motions of the operators. Highly trained analysts time the motions of employees to identify the most economical ways of performing the task and to establish a reasonable standard time for doing it. Synchronized motion pictures of the operators at work are another commonly used technique, from which the analysts can study the efficiency of the motions used.

This idea of identifying the most effective way to do something has been applied in many other situations. Office operations have been analyzed to find the most efficient work movements, timing, postures, and layout. Even salesmen have been studied to determine how they can use their time to better advantage. Stop watches are not necessary in these situations, but the principle of studying the activities performed on a time basis is used to advantage.

Although you will probably never have the opportunity to become a qualified time and motion technician, you can be aware of situations in your own unit where such specialists could help you increase job efficiency. Asking a management specialist to review your operations for possible application of such studies demonstrates your alertness and may result in an opportunity for you to learn more about the method. In addition, you can always study the movements of workers and their timing from a common-sense point of view. It is not difficult to spot the slow or the awkward workers if you are looking for such conditions.

Task improvement

Most of the improvements in the way an individual employee does his work result from a cooperative effort between the employee and his supervisor. Because you have this supervisory responsibility, it will pay you to review how you might approach this job study. Assuming that you have selected a specific position for investigation and the employee concerned is in a favorable frame of mind, the following steps are usually followed.

Identifying the task. It is obviously impossible to improve all parts of a job at once. Selecting a particular task to be studied is not difficult. Previous observation of the job may have given a hint as to where a change would be beneficial. The employee may have given a clue by his questions or by his difficulties in a particular aspect of his work. It usually pays to start with something that is sufficiently time consuming to permit substantial savings. This is often a repetitive task and may well be one that is performed by several employees. In the latter case, the improvement can be used by all the group.

Analyzing the task. After choosing your point of attack, you must find out exactly what is going on. To do this, you use the task analysis or a simple breakdown of what is happening. It consists of jotting down on the left side of a sheet of paper the main steps the operator uses to get the task accomplished as they occur. Any significant notes on how the steps are performed are entered at the right. When completed it would look like this:

TASK ANALYSIS

Place: Auto Maintenance Shop   Task: Demount Wheel *

Supervisor: John Smith   Date: May 14

MAIN STEPS	KEY POINTS
1. Position car	Should there be a specific place for this work?
2. Block wheels	Is this necessary? Why not use hand hydraulic jack so no slippage is possible?
3. Position jack	Where? (Be specific for front and rear wheels.)
4. Raise car	Check on jacks in shop. Are some too slow for this operation?
5. Remove hubcap	What is best tool to use to prevent marring cap or scratching hands?
6. Remove first nut, repeat until all free	Any gain by loosening all nuts first, then spinning off one after another? Try out.
7. Remove wheel	Look into new gadget that raises wheel slightly to prevent accidents.

* NOTE: This is for illustration only; normally the task would be Changing Tire.

To be sure they have covered every major step, most supervisors observe the employee as he performs the work or even do it themselves. Trying to reconstruct the steps from memory is almost certain to result in omissions or incorrect order. The key points entered on the right side represent thoughts that may be of value in making the improvements, such as time, delays, distances, or questions to be answered later.

Questioning each step. Up to this point all you have done is set down a record of what goes on in performing the task, plus any significant ideas on how it is being done. Now you can ask yourself if there is a better way.

The inexperienced supervisor may have difficulty in looking at the task as a whole and trying to visualize some improvement. It is much easier to stimulate the flow of ideas by concentrating on each step, one at a time. The simplest approach is to use the same kind of questions suggested earlier in connection with the informal method of improving work processes. They are reviewed here in a little more detail.

Why is this step necessary? What is its real purpose? Can it be eliminated.

When and where should it be done? Should its sequence or place of operation be changed? Could it be combined with another step to advantage? Could it be performed better as part of another task?

Who should be doing it? Is the present operator the right person? Does he have the necessary skill? Should it be assigned to a more competent person? Could it be given to a less-skilled, and less-expensive employee?

How is it being performed? Is there a better way? Are movements awkward or tiring? Would the use of jigs, fixtures, or other holding devices help? Could performance be improved by changing the arrangement?

By finding answers to such questions, you are almost certain to get some sound ideas for improving the work method. They can be applied to any kind of operation: office, shop, store, laboratory, warehouse, or field trip. It is easy to teach employees to analyze their own assignments in this way and get the satisfaction of making their own job improvements.

Discussing with others. It is a natural tendency to jump to the conclusion that your first suggestions are the best ones. This is not always true. It usually pays to talk over your ideas with other people: you boss, the employees involved, or possibly a management specialist. Some of the reasons are:

To be sure the suggestions will actually accomplish the improvement you anticipate

To prevent the changes causing other difficulties you may not have foreseen

To be sure everyone concerned understands why the change is being made

To secure full acceptance of the ideas both by the employees who will use them and the superior who will evaluate the results

To be certain you have the authority to make the changes, particularly if they involve new costs or affect other work areas

Trying out the new method. When there is substantial agreement that the proposed improvement is worthwhile, you should try it out without delay. Sometimes, of course, the employees may have to be trained in the new method, but this seldom takes long. Often it is possible to plan a trial run before making the final change. This provides an opportunity to locate and eliminate any rough spots. When you have demonstrated the practicability of the change, it can be installed with confidence that the work will be improved.

OTHER TECHNIQUES OF WORK IMPROVEMENT

At several points in the preceding paragraphs reference was made to other techniques used in work improvement. You

can use some of them to good advantage even though you are
not a trained management specialist or production engineer.
You should know about others in case you or someone else
decide that they would be helpful in your operations.

Work measurement

The basic reason for improving work methods is to get more
accomplished with less effort or expense. But if you do not
know how much is being turned out, you cannot tell whether
or not there has been any gain. So, you must have some way
to measure the volume of operations.

In some jobs it is standard practice to maintain a count of
the items completed. If there are tangible units of work, such
as parts processed in a shop, it is relatively easy to keep track
of the quantity. Production records take care of this in terms
of units completed, ton-miles moved, or cases settled. In other
types of work, it is difficult to find work units that represent
production without getting into a complicated record system
that costs more than it is worth. It is interesting to note that the
Wage and Hour Law states *professional* work must be of such
a character that the output produced or the result accomplished
cannot be standardized in relation to a given period of time.
You, your secretary, or a research specialist may not turn out
products that can be counted as measures of all you do.

In these cases, sometimes the best thing to do is to use the
time worked (man-hours) as the measure of accomplishment.
But, it may be possible to use other, more indirect, ways to
measure productivity. For instance, one firm believed it was
desirable to have some estimate of the production of a writer
assigned to prepare guidance materials. Each pamphlet required research and involved rather unpredictable difficulties
in composition. A simple method of measuring accomplishment

was derived. When each unit was assigned, an agreement was reached with the writer as to the number of man-hours needed to complete it, and target date was set. If anything happened during the writing to slow down or speed up the work, the date was changed accordingly. Over a period of time, repeated failure to meet the deadlines led to suspicion of inefficient work habits. A study of the methods being used brought a number of improvements and increased productivity.

This example points out there is a close relationship between the quantity of work performed and the time taken to do it. In a laboratory, 480 analyses were made in a month. The succeeding month only 400 were handled. This looked like a drop in efficiency until it was discovered that the director had only about half the effective manpower the second month because of illness and several resignations. Actually, efficiency was much higher.

Work count can be used for many purposes besides methods improvement. It is valuable to schedule work, to locate bottlenecks, to substantiate personnel needs, to create job enthusiasm, and to evaluate performance. Some of the more technical methods used for this purpose are:

Time study. Accurate measurement of work motions from which engineered standards can be developed

Statistical work measurement. Method by which average data are secured through a scientific sampling process

Predetermined standards. Results of studies to find reasonably approximate performance goals.

These methods are being used to an increasing extent by management specialists for work measurement. The term "performance analysis" is used to describe the total process. In industrial-type operations, methods time measurement, basic motion time study, and work factor techniques are utilized.

The layout and work flow chart

Probably everyone uses a layout chart from time to time, particularly when a move from one location to another is contemplated. In its simplest form, it consists of a scale drawing of the floor space, usually on graph paper. After the area is laid out, it is possible to sketch in all the items (also in scale) that occupy floor space. Sometimes cutout templates of the desks, files, chairs, benches, or machines are used and moved around to find the best arrangement. Obviously, it is more economical to change pencil sketches or paper templates than to move equipment. To arrive at the most satisfactory layout arrangement, several practices are used:

1. Review the work operations from the point of view of the distances employees will have to walk to get their work done. Actual lines can be drawn and distances computed. It may be possible to rearrange and reduce unnecessary movement.

2. Review the flow of work through the unit to see if distances can be reduced, delays eliminated, or actions simplified. If lines are drawn on the chart with arrows to show direction, you get a work flow layout chart such as Figure 9a.

Questions such as the following are asked and answered:

Are the work stations of employees whose activities are closely related placed as conveniently as possible?

Is equipment for general use properly placed?

Are work stations and equipment properly placed with regard to light, safety, traffic, and similar factors?

A study of the physical use of space and the routes taken by people, papers, or parts during the processing of work can be helpful in eliminating unnecessary movement, backtracking,

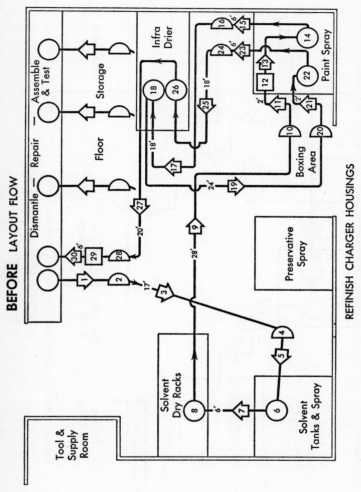

BEFORE LAYOUT FLOW

REFINISH CHARGER HOUSINGS
Figure 9a

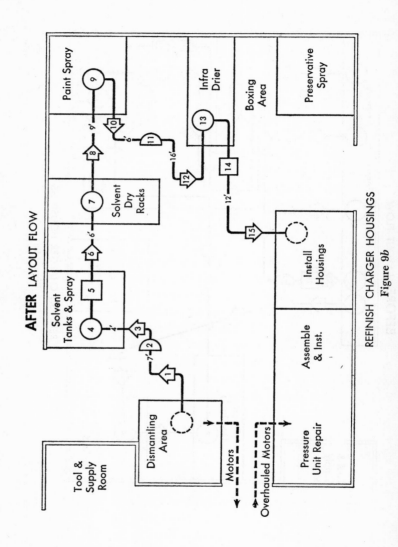

AFTER LAYOUT FLOW

Tool & Supply Room

Dismantling Area

Solvent Tanks & Spray

Solvent Dry Racks

Paint Spray

Infra Drier

Boxing Area

Preservative Spray

Pressure Unit Repair

Assemble & Inst.

Install Housings

Motors

Overhauled Motors

REFINISH CHARGER HOUSINGS
Figure 9b

or congestion. In making such a review, the following suggestions should be helpful:

Employees having the most frequent contact should be close together.

Files and materials should be located for convenient access by those who use them.

Work should follow straight lines without cross travel and backtracking.

Employees who meet the public should be located near entrances.

The best-lighted space should be used for work requiring concentration and close attention.

The work distribution chart

In studying the work of your unit as a whole, you need a more careful analysis than is possible by the informal method or use of a work flow chart. Supervisors frequently find portraying the work of a unit on a distribution chart pays real dividends. Even if no startling work improvements occur, the study will result in a far better understanding of what is going on. Essentially there are only four steps involved, using either a sheet of plain paper ruled as you proceed or a form similar to that shown in Figure 10.

1. Identify the activities in the unit.
   a. Make a list of all the activities or major functions of the unit.
   b. Enter these activities in order along the left-hand side of the paper.
   c. At the right, make a column for each employee who works in the unit.
2. Fill in the chart.
   a. Under each name, write down the specific tasks the

WORK DISTRIBUTION CHART

ORGANIZATIONAL UNIT: Fluid Charger-Rebuilt Unit

APPROVED BY: R. B. Buckter

DATE:

☑ EXISTING
☐ RECOMMENDED

CHARTED BY: John Wilson

ACT. NO.	ACTIVITY	WORK COUNT	HRS. PER WEEK	NAME J. M. WILSON — POSITION EQUIP-MECH LDR. — GRADE WB-16: TASKS	WORK COUNT	HRS. PER WEEK	NAME A. R. CLYDE — POSITION EQUIP-MECH. — GRADE WB-14: TASKS	WORK COUNT	HRS. PER WEEK
1	DISMANTLE CHARGERS		57	[illegible]		1 1½ 1½	[illegible]		1 2 2
2	OVERHAUL CHARGER PRESSURE UNITS		69	[illegible]		4 1½ 3½ 3	[illegible]		6 4 4 4
3	REFINISH CHARGER HOUSINGS		41						
4	REMOUNT CHARGERS		65½	[illegible]		2 2 4½ 1	[illegible]		3 3 4 2
5	PROCESS CHARGERS FOR PRESERVATION		26						
6	SUPERVISION AND ADMINISTRATION		17½	[illegible]		4½ ½ ½ 4½ 1½	[illegible]		2
7	MISCELLANEOUS		24	[illegible]		1 2	[illegible]		2 1
	TOTALS		280			40			40

ACT. NO.	NAME T. F. OMEARS — POSITION EQUIP-MECH. — GRADE WB-12: TASKS	WORK COUNT	HRS. PER WEEK	NAME A. R. COLINDA — POSITION EQUIP-MECH. — GRADE WB-12: TASKS	WORK COUNT	HRS. PER WEEK	NAME J. S. GARCIA — POSITION UTILITY MAN — GRADE WB-8: TASKS	WORK COUNT	HRS. PER WEEK
1	[illegible]		1 2 2	[illegible]		1 2 2	[illegible]		4
2	[illegible]		6 1 4 5	[illegible]		6 1 4 5	[illegible]		1 2½
3							[illegible]		5½ 14 1
4	[illegible]		3 4 5 2	[illegible]		3 4 5 2	[illegible]		1 2
5	[illegible]		1 2	[illegible]		1 2	[illegible]		1 2 3
6	[illegible]		2	[illegible]		2			
7							[illegible]		1 2
TOTALS			40			40			40

ACT. NO.	NAME G. R. WALE — POSITION UTILITY MAN — GRADE WB-8: TASKS	WORK COUNT	HRS. PER WEEK	NAME M. X. QUIROL — POSITION LABORER — GRADE WB-3: TASKS	WORK COUNT	HRS. PER WEEK
1	[illegible]		4	[illegible]		10
2	[illegible]		1 2½			
3	[illegible]		5½ 14 1			
4	[illegible]		1 2	[illegible]		10
5	[illegible]		2 3	[illegible]		6 3
6						
7	[illegible]		2 2	[illegible]		6 5
TOTALS			40			40

Figure 10

person performs in connection with eac
tivities.

b. If an employee has no part in an activity,
block empty.

c. At the right, enter the number of man-hours
he spends on that task.

d. Add vertically to make sure that the total time
week is accounted for. If you are short, some
and possibly some activities, have been overlo
If you have too many hours, the estimates shoul
revised.

e. When all the columns are completed, add horizonta
to find total time spent by the group on each acti
ity.

3. Analyze the chart. Here you have a list of the total tasks
and activities of the unit in one place, together with the
contribution in hours that each employee is making
toward carrying them out. To get full value from this
information, questions similar to the following are considered. The need to change individual assignments
becomes evident as the items are questioned.

a. What activities take the most time? Should they take
the most time? What is the contribution of each employee? Note for future study activities involving
several steps. (For further analysis you may want to
use the process chart technique that follows.)

b. Is there any misdirected effort? Is too much time
spent on unimportant tasks or even unnecessary ones?

c. Are skills being used properly? Is everyone doing the
tasks he can do best? Are special skills and abilities
going to waste?

d. Are employees doing too many unrelated tasks? Is
efficiency and enthusiasm hampered and fatigue in-

creased by assignment of too many unrelated tasks to one employee? Is time lost in frequent change-over from one kind of work to another?

e. Are tasks spread too thinly? Are too many people doing the same thing, resulting in inconsistency, needless interruptions, and "buck-passing"?

f. Is work distributed evenly? Do some people have too great a work load, and others not enough? Are willing employees overworked?

If these questions are asked and answered honestly, ideas for improving procedures will usually result. Many times the suggestion is so simple and so obvious that you wonder why you did not think of it long before. In these cases, the changes can be made at once. In other instances, however, you get only a hint that improvement is possible and have to make further detailed studies to be certain the idea is practical. If a long procedure is involved, you may use the process chart, discussed in the next part of this chapter.

4. Make the desired changes. After you have identified the places where a change appears beneficial, you should assure yourself of the improvements you actually want to make. Three hints are in order at this point:

a. Make haste slowly, be sure all the factors have been considered.

b. Talk the proposed change over with the employees concerned; they may have some good ideas.

c. When a change proves to be desirable, do not delay to make it.

The process chart

The layout and work distribution charts take a picture of work as it is at a given time similar to a still photograph. Because many operations involve a whole series of related tasks, each of which takes time, you need a method to show these processes, that is, something like a motion picture. Just as a movie of an actor crossing a room shows each separate step distinctly, so the process chart shows every step in work as it progresses, such as the movement of a paper in administrative work or the progressive steps in assembling a meter. Study of the two preceding charts may give you hints of processes where further analysis would pay dividends.

As an aid to studies of this kind, symbols have been devised to help visualize the types of action that are occurring. Five of these are used:

Operation. This word has been used previously in a general sense. Here, it specifically means an action when an object is intentionally changed, worked upon, assembled, modified, or prepared. It includes making a plan and giving or receiving information.

Transportation. This refers to any movement of the object from one place to another, other than movements during an operation.

Inspection. This is the examination or checking of the object for quality or quantity of accomplishment.

Delay. This means situations in which the object is being held without action for further processing.

Storage. This refers to safeguarding and protecting an object from unauthorized removal.

These symbols are often printed on the flow process chart form (Figure 11) to assist the analyst in visualizing what is happening in the process.

FLOW PROCESS CHART

NUMBER	9 B
PAGE NO.	1
NO. OF PAGES	1

PROCESS: REFINISH HOUSINGS PRESSURE FLUID CHARGER

MAN OR ☐ / MATERIAL [X]

CHART BEGINS: DISMANTLING RACK
CHART ENDS: ASSEMBLY BENCH

CHARTED BY: WILSON
DATE: 3 DEC 1960

ORGANIZATION: PRESSURE UNIT RECONDITIONING LIGHT EQUIPMENT SHOP

DETAILS OF: PRESENT [X] METHOD / PROPOSED ☐ METHOD

SUMMARY

ACTIONS	PRESENT NO.	PRESENT TIME	PROPOSED NO.	PROPOSED TIME	DIFFERENCE NO.	DIFFERENCE TIME
OPERATIONS ◯	6					
TRANSPORTATIONS ⇧	15					
INSPECTIONS ☐	2					
DELAYS D	7	190				
STORAGES ▽	0					
DISTANCE TRAVELED (Feet)	166					

Details

#	DETAILS OF PRESENT METHOD	DISTANCE IN FEET	TIME	WHY? WHAT?	WHY? WHERE?	WHY? WHEN?	WHY? WHO?	WHY? HOW?	ELIMINATE	COMBINE	SEQUENCE	PLACE	PERSON	IMPROVE	NOTES
1	FROM DISMANTLING TO RACK	6													
2	HOUSING ON RACK		30		X			X	X	X					CAN RACK BE MOVED TO CLEANER AREA?
3	TO SOLVENT CLEANER AREA	17				X				X		X			
4	ON FLOOR STACK		30							X					WHY ?
5	TO SOLVENT TANKS AND SPRAY	4			X			X	X	X					
6	PRESSURE CLEANED WITH SOLVENT														
7	TO DRY RACK	6			X		X								
8	ON DRY RACK														
9	TO PAINT SPRAY AREA	28						X							
10	ON FLOOR		15						X						

226

Figure 11 — Flow Process Chart

No.	Activity	Value	Remarks
11	TO BENCH	2	
12	DETERMINES RUST OR CORROSION CHECKED (REJECTS TO WASTE)		BY PAINT SPRAY OPERATOR
13	TO PAINT SPRAY	3	
14	SPRAY INSIDE OF HOUSING		BOTH UTILITY MEN DO PAINTING
15	TO TRUCK RACK	6	
16	ON TRUCK RACK	30	
17	4 HOUSINGS TO INFRA DRIER	18	
18	DRY IN HEATER 1 HOUR		
19	TO PAINT SPRAY	24	
20	ON FLOOR	15	
21	TO SPRAY BENCH	2	
22	SPRAY OUTSIDE		CAN INSIDE AND OUTSIDE TO BE PAINTED AT SAME TIME?
23	TO TRUCK RACK	6	
24	ON TRUCK RACK	18 / 30	
25	4 HOUSINGS TO INFRA DRIER		
26	DRY IN HEATER 1 HOUR		
27	TO ASSEMBLY	20	
28	ON FLOOR AT ASSEMBLY	40	
29	INSPECTS INSIDE AND OUTSIDE		INSPECTED BY MECHANIC
30	TO ASSEMBLY BENCH	6	REJECTS TO SPRAY BOOTH

Figure 11

227

Making a process analysis

Essentially, the process chart technique is similar to that used in task analysis, except that here you are concerned with the flow of work between members of the work force rather than with the actions of an individual employee. You do, however, break down the process into main steps (details) and key points (notes) in two columns. In summary, the method is as follows:

1. Record the present process.
   a. After selecting the process to be studied, decide where to begin and where to stop. Do not attempt too much at one time.
   b. Write down what happens, step by step, in the order in which events occur.
   c. Opposite each step involving transportation, enter the distance of movement and, opposite each storage, the time before it moves.
   d. Add up the number of storages and delays, the time involved, the transportation and distance, the number of inspections, and the number of operations. The results are now ready to be studied for possible improvements.
2. Analyze the data. Filling out the chart has probably in itself raised some questions as to time involved, sequence, distances, or method used. As in all work improvement, you have to apply your pattern of questioning to each step in proper order.
   a. Why is this step necessary? What does it contribute? What is its purpose?
   b. Where should this step be done? Can it be done

easier, in less time by changing the location of the employee or the equipment?

c. When should it be done? Is it in the right sequence? Can I combine and simplify by moving it ahead or back?

d. Who should do it? Is the right person handling it or is it more logical to assign it to someone else?

e. How is the job being done? Would different equipment or layout help? How can it be made easier?

Seeking answers to these inquiries will bring to light parts of the process where you might be able to secure greater efficiency. You should give particular attention to time spent in getting work ready or putting it away and unnecessary delays or storage. Similarly, you should try to eliminate or reduce movements of the work or workers, combine steps where possible, and thus simplify the whole process.

3. Make the changes. The questioning applied to each step of the process will naturally lead to suggestions for worthwhile changes. Unless you actually make the changes, you have wasted your time. However, a manager should be fairly certain his recommendations or decisions are sound before he acts. As a check, it is often helpful to fill out a process chart of the proposed method so you and others can study it in detail step by step, before going into the expenditure of time, effort, or money to install the new plan. When you are reasonably certain that you have made as much improvement as possible at this time and have secured the necessary authority, the changes should be made promptly.

Using the technique

As already implied, nearly everyone makes some use of work measurement and of layout charts. There is no reason why you cannot also learn to use the work distribution chart to improve work. The more you practice these three methods, the more skillful you will become in their use and the more improvements that will result. The process chart is more difficult to apply skillfully. Unless you have been trained in its use, it is advisable to secure the assistance of a methods analyst. Training in the use of all these devices may be available through a work simplification training program. If it is, you would be wise to arrange to attend the sessions.

EVALUATING THE CHANGE

Regardless of the method used to make a work improvement, you should be certain the change is really beneficial. Therefore, you need to check on the results after the improvement is made. Two questions may well be asked.

Is the improvement actually in effect?

After working many hours to improve a process and apparently having it accepted by everyone concerned, you may be surprised to find employees are continuing to work the same old way. Possibly they were not thoroughly sold on the change, they may not have gotten around to it yet, or they may just be resistant to change. Regardless of the reason, it pays to make sure the new plan is getting a fair trial.

Is the improvement actually effective?

Everyone is inclined to be proud of his own brain-child and to think it cannot fail. You may assume the change is producing all the results you claimed for it, while in actual practice it may even be slowing up operations. Everyone has probably had an experience where, despite all careful calculations, the improvement simply did not improve anything. Naturally, you want to be among the first to know about such a situation. Possibly only a minor correction is needed. Maybe the whole plan was poorly conceived. Surely it is better to make prompt adjustments, even going back to the original process, than to insist the new procedures be followed when everyone recognizes they are ineffective.

If the improvement turns out to be all that was expected, you want to know that too. Nothing does more to make your job really satisfying than to know you have made valuable work improvements.

Normally, such studies result in increased productivity, less waste, and lower costs of operation. These are the results you want. It is well to remember, however, that in focusing your attention on the work you cannot disregard the workers. Regardless of how mechanically correct your new methods may be, they will not result in improvement unless the employees actually carry them out as intended.

Even when employees accept the changes wholeheartedly and fully cooperate in carrying them out, there are times when productivity is not increased. Recent studies have disclosed that work can be too completely mechanized. People are not automatons or robots who can continue to make routine movements indefinitely. Both monotony and fatigue enter in. People produce more and better work if they are permitted a reasonable opportunity to break the pace occasionally, to move around, and to change tasks. These factors are of real significance in over-all job efficiency because they consider the human element in production.

SUMMARY

The free enterprise system includes the idea of competition as a prominent factor in the economy. Better products and better ways of making them expand markets and reduce prices charged the consumers. In this respect, every business is subject to the threat of competitive practices. Managers must be alert to the possibilities of work improvement if they are to contribute effectively to the success of their own business operations. To this end, executives and supervisors study the work of the organization as performed either in group activity or by individual employees.

Because few men can discharge managerial responsibilities competently and at the same time develop skill in the more complex work improvement techniques described in this chapter, increasing use is made of specialists to secure increased efficiency. Managers, however, must have at least a general knowledge of these methods, as applied by the technicians, to be able to make use of them most effectively.

12

Management Tomorrow

The preceding chapters implied that good managers are intelligent, considerate persons who understand both the theory and practice of their professions. Even though some supervisors and executives fail to meet these standards, as a group, businessmen are becoming better executives. Literally thousands are taking courses, reading books, attending management conferences, and then trying to practice sound management on the job. Several significant trends are emerging as business leaders work at self-improvement. This final chapter covers some of the areas where progress is being made.

MORAL RESPONSIBILITY

Any review of the dynamics of modern management would be incomplete without reference to a change in the manager's attitude toward society. Current literature is replete with attempts to define more clearly what might be called "the ethics of management." This movement is the culmination of a developing philosophy that deserves careful attention. As Harold F. Smiddy, Vice-President of Management Consultation Services at General Electric, pointed out, these new concepts "do not come from academic adventures in a philosophic ivory tower" but from the "cold and factual experience of business and industrial history." [1]

Big business

Historically, management was based mainly on power and authority stemming from the rights of ownership. This was changed by the industrial revolution which ushered in an economic era that made mechanical power available for industrial uses wherever needed. Because considerable capital investment was required for business operations, the foundation was laid for big business and the corporate form of organization. The authority of ownership was passed on to thousands of stockholders. Today, management is largely exercised by employees who make professions of their jobs.

During the same period, workers were organizing into labor unions which, over the years, matched big business in strength and bargaining power. The resultant labor negotiations and laws to eliminate or minimize inequities on either side also brought changes in management practices.

Management began to realize that the operations of big business play a significant part in the total national economy and what benefits the country also benefits the company: It is good business to be ethical. With this realization, corporation planning started to consider not only the stockholders but also the employees, the customers, and the public. This evolutionary process has taken business a long way from the old philosophy of *caveat emptor* or "let the buyer beware."

[1] *Integrating and Motivating for Effective Performance*, General Electric Co., New York, 1955, p. 6.

Employee relations

The social responsibility assumed by business is exemplified in the current widespread interest in "human relations." It is more than a popular topic for discussion at conventions and meetings. Large corporations are investing heavily in both time and money, training supervisors to establish and maintain satisfactory relations with subordinate employees.

For the most part, these efforts by business are the result of a desire to uncover the best methods to resolve differences. There is a widespread agreement that it is to everyone's advantage to arrive at mutual understanding and cooperation; misunderstandings, opposition, and antagonism are costly.

If supervisors knew how each man would respond, they could easily work out a formula for each situation, and employee relations could be reduced to a mechanical selection of the correct stimulus to get the desired response. Actually, some training programs fall into this trap by trying to provide pat solutions or "right" answers to human problems.

However, even though people have many characteristics in common, they also differ from each other radically; the democratic concepts used in business are based on the recognition of individual differences. The whole hazy area of human relations is being studied scientifically to learn why people behave, or misbehave, as they do, and many of these findings are useful to executives who must have their goals carried out by others. But, because there are few blueprints in human relations that can be followed blindly, executives generally have to rely on mature judgment to gauge their actions with each situation.

Fortunately, human beings are adaptable. They can learn

new skills and, with proper incentives, can act as a team to get a task performed. If they are provided with considerate leadership, individuals will forego their own separate goals and ambitions, at least temporarily, and cooperate to achieve a common objective. This kind of efficient group action reflects sound management.

Codes of ethics

An increasing number of business leaders are stating that there are such things as principles and ideals in business. As mentioned earlier, it is no longer unusual for a firm to place public good ahead of private gain and conduct business in ways that benefit the community; big business is well aware of the effect of its operations on the economy. Many business associations have even formulated codes of ethics that are generally well observed, and infractions by employees frequently result in disciplinary action.

Paul Garrett, a Vice-President at General Motor Corp., puts it this way, "Industry stands for the good life, for the social and economic betterment of all, for the proposition to produce more with the same amount of human effort is a sound social and economic objective. Industry's position in this respect rests squarely upon the ethical and moral concept of the dignity of the individual." [2]

Professor Harold B. Wess, of American University, made much of the same implication in an address before the Foreign Service Institute of the Department of State. He stated that American businessmen could give the rest of the world a technology and managerial know-how, fully aware of the spiritual values involved and the innate dignity of man.

[2] Public Relations Journal, October, 1956.

Leadership being redefined

American management is redefining its concept of leadership as part of this period of self-inquiry. The quality of leadership is now being judged on attitude and action rather than authority.

An executive reveals much of his real character in his attitude toward his associates and particularly toward his subordinates. "Does he show disdain or contempt toward those in less fortunate positions? Is he influenced by differences in race, religion, or political affiliation? Does he really try to be fair in his dealings with others? Does he sincerely try to belong to the group and contribute to it rather than dominate it? Is he overly impressed by prestige, social standing, or financial resources?" The answers to these and similar questions are definite indicators of a man's character.

Actions are even more significant. "How does the executive conduct himself in a group of business associates? Does he attempt to dominate the situation? Does he attempt to influence others into accepting his ideas or does he listen to and respect their opinions? Does he have an open mind or only seek confirmation of his own views?" What he does is often far more significant than what he says in his leadership role.

Integration of goals

Many years ago, Mary Parker Follett [3] pointed out that problems or disagreements can be resolved in three ways. The first is by authority: The person in command makes a

[3] H. C. Metcalf and L. Urwich (eds.), "Dynamic Administration: The Collected Papers of Mary Parker Follett," Harper and Brothers, New York, 1941.

decision which those under him are to follow. The second is by compromise: Each party or side gives up part of its wishes. In either case, some of the persons concerned, often most of them, are not entirely satisfied with the solution because they failed to get all or part of their goals. Sometimes, no one is satisfied with the results. The third possibility, which is more satisfactory, is being used more often in business and industry as executives search for better ways to achieve management goals. This method is problem-solving by integration. The wishes of everyone concerned are integrated so the decision satisfies everyone. Such solutions are not easily achieved and require a high degree of management competence.

The concept has been expressed in many different ways. Harold Smiddy actually uses the word "integrating" to describe the practice at General Electric. Dr. Hurst R. Anderson, President of American University, termed it "Ethical Values in Administration" in an address before the Society for Personnel Administration. O. M. Ohmann also discussed the ethics of management in his article, "Skyhooks—with Special Implications for Monday Through Friday." [4]

RESEARCH FINDINGS

Both the quantity and the quality of current research in business management are impressive. Prominent universities such as Ohio State, Southern California, and University of Chicago are making valuable contributions. Private enterprise also is assisting substantially not only by subsidizing research in professional institutions but by carrying on studies within their own organizations.

Possibly some of the most important research for students of management is that which has been conducted over the past

[4] *Harvard Business Review,* May–June, 1955.

several years in the University of Michigan's Institute for Social Research. These studies present ample proof that the most successful executives are not those who depend solely on a cold mechanistic application of the principles of management. Instead, the effective manager seeks to combine the appropriate principles of scientific management with the great power of those major motivations that influence human behavior.

This does not mean that good management is skillful manipulation of subordinates. In fact, workers usually sense when they are being manipulated and react negatively. As Wayne G. Broehl, Jr., of the Amos Tuck School of Business Administration at Dartmouth College, pointed out: "It is remarkable how quickly and intuitively subordinates can sense a man's ethics . . . firm and lasting human relations can be effected only through application of principles within an ethical framework." [5] An honest relationship of confidence and mutual respect between the supervisor and his subordinates is needed to increase productivity.

Research findings also indicate that persons in managerial positions need far more maturity and wisdom in dealing with others now than was required with the traditional forms of management. They cannot expect efficient operations if they treat employees as only a means to get the work done. Good managers understand people and supply them with appropriate goals and satisfactions in the work situation. Dr. Rensis Likert, director of the Institute for Social Research at the University of Michigan, describes it by saying "when the worker . . . feels that his boss sees him only as an instrument of production, as merely a cog in a machine, he is likely to be a poor producer. However, when he feels that his boss is genu-

[5] Dunn's Review, May, 1957.

inely interested in him, his problems, his future, and his well-being, he is more likely to be a high producer." [6]

Group dynamics

The findings of the group dynamics movement give another significant aspect of leadership. Study in this area has determined that there are three forces operating when people work to accomplish a common purpose, and, more important, the relative strength of these forces can be modified by the quality of leadership.

The first force is *group attainment*. This represents the desire to get along with the purpose of the meeting, to move toward the common goal, to progress, or generally to accomplish something.

The second motivating factor is *group cohesion*. This is shown in the tendency of people to occupy themselves with what is happening within the group, the backgrounds of other members, developing understanding, resolution of differences, and with happiness or unhappiness in the group situation. Workers no longer act as isolated individuals spurred by the incentive of higher wages. Today, they are members of a team. At General Electric, the teamwork idea is clearly expressed in the company's philosophy that any job has two aspects: The work an employee does himself and the relation of his activities with the work of others.

The third force is *empathy* or the degree to which the leader or group members can put themselves in the other fellow's shoes. It signifies the ability to become aware of what others are thinking and why. Supervisors who develop sensitivity to the feelings of their associates usually obtain higher

---

[6] *Motivation: The Core of Management*, American Management Assn., New York, 1953, p. 5.

levels of efficiency and morale than those who are concerned primarily with performance schedules.

The time-honored practices of dealing with subordinates solely on an individual basis is disappearing, however. Dr. Likert states the principle this way: "The greater the skill in using group methods of supervision, the greater are the productivity and job satisfaction." [7] He goes on to say that "effective leadership is characterized by sincere concern for the employee as an individual and acceptance of him as a full-member of the team." [8]

These are only a few descriptions of what businessmen hope are better methods of management, where the desires, hopes, and aspirations of the diverse elements of an organization are integrated into a solution satisfactory to everyone.

Creative thinking

Another trend in modern management is the movement to promote creative thinking. Expressed by such different phrases as creativity, creative problem-solving, creative engineering, or applied imagination, creative thinking has been used in many diverse places, ranging from the Air Force ROTC program, or the Massachusetts Institute of Technology, to the AC Spark Plug Division of General Motors.

Dr. J. P. Guilford of the University of Southern California [9] and other psychologists have pointed out that although nearly everyone has creative impulses, these impulses can be blocked effectively by doubt, fear of ridicule, or laziness. The significant aspect is that, even so, creativity can be "taught." A number of universities have had creative problem-solving in-

[7] *Motivation: The Core of Management*, American Management Assn., New York, 1953, p. 6.

[8] *Ibid.*, p. 38.

[9] See Chapter 2.

stitutes and literally hundreds of universities, colleges, and adult education programs offer courses in creativity.

Virtually all of the largest corporations in the United States offer some training to selected groups of employees in how to use the imagination. For example, General Foods Corp., Armstrong Cork Co., Du Pont, and United States Steel Corp. all have programs in creative thinking, brainstorming, or both. General Electric has been using creative problem-solving successfully since 1937. One U.S. Steel plant has presented a course in creative thinking to 1400 staff members, who, upon completion, form brainstorming teams to train other employees. Privately operated concerns, such as the Creative Education Foundation, Inc. (see p. 54), are taxed to supply business with information about how to apply the powers of imagination profitably. Some supervisors still resist the techniques of creative thinking, but in general, business and industry are finding a wealth of profit-making ideas in their employees.

Motivation

As pointed out several times earlier, although this book is primarily concerned with managing *work*, management of the *work force* is equally important. The Management Cycle chart (see p. 14) shows the human element as central in the phases of work management. Actually, successful businessmen consider all of their resources: conceptual, human, and material.

A current trend in management emphasizes ways to motivate workers to reach the desired degree of work efficiency. Although they are primarily concerned with getting the work accomplished effectively, executives are beginning to realize the best way to do so is with the full support of employees. To be successful executives, students of work management must also be students of personnel management. This does not mean the essential management processes should be replaced with an all-out drive to motivate workers. Supervisors should continue to use the tried and proved methods but also give equal attention to the people involved.

Managers are becoming increasingly aware of the tremendous abilities that are latent in people. The impact of the leader on total group accomplishment is being reaffirmed by research in group behavior. Although even more research is needed in this area, it is generally accepted that the leader has an ethical responsibility to motivate the activities of his group. A manager must give satisfactory reasons for doing the work and have these reasons accepted by the workers to provide the incentive necessary for increased production. The job becomes worthwhile when the aims and aspirations of one person are shared and assisted by the others,[10] but this requires a full understanding of organizational goals and the desire to fulfill them.

The results of research in this area have only recently become available for day-to-day use. Now, supervisors are beginning to understand how to use these forces to give employees the satisfaction of real accomplishment. In doing so, the work is done more efficiently, and the employees develop their capabilities and feel personal accomplishment. This approach requires clear communication, guidance, opportunities for growth, and the removal of obstacles. Peter Drucker called it "management by objective" in contrast to management by authority.

These emerging concepts demand new skills, human insights, and spiritual depth from leadership. Donald and Eleanor Laird summarized the principles by saying that "the successful leader operates by mobilizing the mental and social forces

[10] Pitirim Sorokin, *Explorations in Altruistic Love and Behavior,* The Beacon Press, Boston, 1950, p. 23.

within his followers and heading these forces toward some common goals. He uses methods which create a climate and interactions which make the followers' goals clearer and more personal, more constructive for everybody concerned. And the followers sense that their leader is helping them make headway to reach these goals." [11]

SUMMARY

A clear pattern of management philosophy has been evolving over the years, culminating in a growing sense of responsibility. The teachings of such leaders as Mary Parker Follett are now being applied in everyday business life. Research shows that the most successful executives have a strong sense of obligation, lead by persuasion, and secure the willing cooperation of their subordinates. They have positive and creative approaches to both their fellow workers and job situations.

Current trends indicate that a more complete understanding of the management processes will better equip the executive and supervisory group to furnish business leadership in the future. Greater understanding of coworkers and superiors, of the responsibility to operate business in the interest of all, and of sound ethical standards will also come with the improved ways to manage work. In the future, managers may achieve greater efficiency, a more complete understanding with all levels of employees, and a more satisfying business life for themselves.

[11] Donald and Eleanor Laird, *The New Psychology for Leadership,* McGraw-Hill Book Co., Inc., New York, 1956, p. 65.